ECCLESIASTES

Survival
in the 21st Century

TOM FINLEY

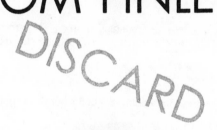

Regal Books
A Division of GL Publications
Ventura, California, U.S.A.

Published by Regal Books
A Division of GL Publications
Ventura, California 93006
Printed in U.S.A.

Library of Congress Cataloging-in-Publication Data applied for

2 3 4 5 6 7 8 9 10 / 93 92 91 90 89

Rights for publishing this book in other languages are contracted by
Gospel Literature International (GLINT) foundation. GLINT also pro-
vides technical help for the adaptation, translation, and publishing of
Bible study resources and books in scores of languages worldwide. For
further information, contact GLINT, Post Office Box 488, Rosemead,
California, 91770, U.S.A., or the publisher.

Contents

To Rick and Lauren Bundschuh:
A life of meaning

Introduction

Have you ever gone spelunking?

Your first thought might be Are you kidding? My mom would kill me! Well, maybe not.

A spelunker is someone who explores caves. Maybe you've had a chance to crawl through a dark, narrow tunnel deep within a mountain—the feeling can be eerie, especially if you've chosen to explore the gloomiest, tiniest recesses.

Or perhaps you've found yourself alone in a particularly ominous forest. The strange animal sounds, the noise of the wind, the feeling of aloneness and the sense of hidden worlds all work in concert to produce a feeling like no other. Excitement! Or fear.

Most people would rather remain in the lighter, brighter parts of the world. But there are those of us who love the adventure of going off the trodden path, who want to experience the new and different and possibly scary. It's the hope of finding something good, some hidden treasure just up ahead.

The Bible, too, has light and shadowy areas. Matthew, Mark, Luke, John, the Epistles—these are the books that make up most of the New Testament. To the majority of young Christians, this part of the Bible is fairly familiar territory. It's well-lit: We study the Gospels and Epistles every week in our youth group Bible studies. But there is another section of the Bible. A mysterious, seldom explored region called the Old Testament. It is made up of the biblical writings done before Jesus was born on earth. Oh, sure, there are some familiar landmarks like Psalms and the stories of Adam and Eve, Noah and Daniel in the lions' den. But for the most part, the Old Testament is like a black cave or an unexplored forest. We tend to avoid it—it seems too deep for us.

Well, let's be adventurers for once. And let's pick the tiniest, gloomiest path we can find. We are looking for hidden gold! And we will find it, too, because God's Word is the richest treasure on earth.

Buried down in the dimmest recesses is a piece of wisdom called Ecclesiastes. Even the name is weird. But we will dig it up and discover great wealth. All it takes is a little time and a desire for wisdom. You must be prepared, however, for a strange trip. The book is not easily understood—in fact, it's easy to misunderstand and to miss the life-changing wisdom it holds. Together, we'll open it up like a treasure chest and share the riches inside. First, though, we need to explore a little bit of background.

The Author
Nowhere in the book is mentioned the name of the author. But several passages suggest that it was King Solomon, David's son. We

cannot be certain that he wrote it, but it seems very safe to assume he did. If it wasn't him, it was certainly someone trying to make it look as if Solomon wrote it—a widely practiced and accepted form of literature in those days.

Solomon is reputed to have been the world's wisest man (see 1 Kings 3:11,12). If you've ever read Ecclesiastes, you may question his wisdom! The book seems to have been written by someone groping in the dark—but a closer examination will reveal that Solomon knew exactly where he was and where he was going. This is part of the hidden treasure that we will discover.

The Purpose

The book has one major theme: Life not centered on God is meaningless and without worth. This is one of those all-time great truths that should be branded on everybody's forehead. Life takes meaning and worth when we are united with our Creator. Apart from Him we can do nothing. Jesus said the same thing in John 15:5.

A secondary theme in Ecclesiastes is the idea that there are limitations on what people can do. Human understanding and achievement can only go so far without God. Mad pursuit of life, meaning and happiness will have less than satisfactory results. Only God can cross the limits, so we must travel with Him if we hope to find real purpose.

The Style

The Old Testament can be divided into several types of writings. Some are histories of what God was doing. Others contain the laws that God set down. There are prophetical writings and even poetry.

Ecclesiastes is the type of book known as wisdom literature. There are two types of wisdom literature found in the Bible: optimistic and pessimistic.

Optimistic wisdom (Proverbs is an example) is basically upbeat sayings about how to win at life: "Do this, and everything will go well for you." Pessimistic wisdom literature is more of a "Woe is me, life is meaningless!" That's Ecclesiastes all over.

God Is Our Meaning

Ecclesiastes 1:1-11

"Meaningless! Meaningless!"
says the Teacher.
"Utterly meaningless!
Everything is meaningless."
Ecclesiastes 1:2

Our hunger for ultimate meaning in life will never be satisfied until we know the living God who has revealed Himself to us in history.

Ecclesiastes is not an easy book to slide through. You show great courage in your willingness to make the effort! Hopefully, your desire is not only to read the book, but to discover potent truths that will make a difference in your life. Ecclesiastes can show you—if you know how to look—truths that can lead you to a life filled with the sort of things everybody wants: happiness, purpose and meaning. The purpose of this book is to teach you how to look.

Before we jump into the thick of things, I want to introduce you to a missionary friend of mine. His name is Mark Nakatsukasa. A very scary thing happened to him at a beach called Acid Drops on the island of Kauai. His story may help you to understand one essential step to unlocking the truths of Ecclesiastes.

Here is Mark's story, given during an interview taped for this book.

Author: Mark, I want to ask you about your experience with the shark.

Mark: It happened like this. My friend Norm and I went surfing at dawn. We paddled out and caught a couple of waves—it was really good surf. I had seen something in the water a little earlier. I told Norm that I either saw a large turtle or a shark fin farther out. But we ignored it. Later on I was stroking for a wave, and just as the wave was picking me up, I was ready to stand up, something hit me from underneath with incredible force. It knocked me clear off my board. I remember flying through the air.

Author: How far did you fly?

Mark: I don't know, but I wasn't just turned over. I was completely out of the water. I landed in the face of the wave. As I was being held under by the force of the wave, I could see the belly of the shark going by me. The shark circled me twice.

Author: How big was the shark?

Mark: At least eight to ten feet. Through my mind flashed all these things that you are supposed to do during a shark attack, but I knew that the only thing I could do was pray. Believe it or not, I had so little faith at the time that I didn't pray that the shark would go away or that God would deliver me, but that God would make it not hurt too badly to be eaten alive!

Author: Ugh!

Mark: That's how little faith I had. So I just closed my eyes and asked the Lord to take me home peacefully. I guess when you come to the end of your rope you are in another world. I felt like I was in the presence of the Lord, waiting for Him to take me home. Then I opened my eyes and realized that the shark was gone. My board (with a large mouth-shaped dent) was sitting on the surface next to me. I saw Norm paddling out to me so I said, "I think we better go in."

Author: What did he say?

Mark: He said, "Good idea!" So we paddled in as fast as we could! Norm had seen the whole thing. He saw me knocked off my board. He saw a tail and fin thrashing though the water. He saw the nose of my board bobbing in the water and he thought the shark was eating me.

Author: Mark, how has your attitude toward sharks changed?

Mark: I had always heard about shark attacks and I knew sharks were dangerous. As a kid I often went deep sea fishing with my dad. Every time we would stop the boat to bottom fish, big, HUGE, sharks would come and scratch their backs on the prop. They would come right up against the side of the boat. Some of them were longer than the boat. You didn't want to hang your hands or feet over the edge—that's how close they were.

But I had grown comfortable with sharks. They are known to eat people, but they never do, I thought. In fact, I go to a surf spot on the North Shore named Kalihiwai that is a breeding ground for sharks. There are sharks all over it in summer. But in winter they are gone, except for one that always hangs around. A white tip. Even during big surf he'll be seen. He'll cruise right into the crowd of surfers. When he's spotted everyone paddles in. He's a really big shark. I used to live right in front of that surf spot and I'd laugh at those guys when they get scared out of the water. I'd say, "I've seen that shark so many times. He never does anyone any harm." So I would stay out surfing while everybody else went in. It was great!

But when the shark attacked me, when he was circling me, I knew that there was nothing I could do against a creature that wanted to eat me.

Author: So your attitude towards sharks changed radically. Suddenly you went from a vague belief that sharks might take a little "sharky lick" now and then to a dynamic fear of sharks.

Mark: For at least two years after the attack, as much as I tried not to be, every time I went in the water I was conscious of sharks. Even now I am always watching for fins. I had tremendous fear. I don't know how many times I asked God to take the fear away. He finally delivered me of it.

Author: Mark, I want the reader to understand that this shark story teaches something important about finding meaning and purpose in life. It seems to me that your experience with the shark knocked out your old devil-may-care attitude toward sharks. Now you have a very healthy respect for them! In the same way, I guess you would say that when a person says he or she believes in God, it should be more than just a mental assent or "Yes, I believe there is some kind of God out there" or "I have no argument against God." Faith should be something stronger and . . .

Mark: Oh, yeah! In fact, for years I was a New Ager. I had a guru and everything. Yet, if you asked me if I believed that Jesus Christ was God, I would say yes. And if you asked if I believed He was the Son of God and He did all the miracles, I would have said, "Yes, I believe all that." And yet, it was all head knowledge. My life was unchanged. I saw no power in Christianity.

But later, when I truly became a Christian, I immediately knew I wanted to serve God, because I had always wanted to serve the real God, I just hadn't known Him. And when I finally experienced a real relationship with Him, there was no doubt in my mind that I should serve Him full-time as a missionary. He's real.

I said at the beginning of the chapter that our hunger for ultimate meaning in life will never be satisfied until we know God. But to know Him means more than just to believe He's out there somewhere. Mark knew sharks were out there, but it made no difference to him. Not until he tangled with one.

This, then, is the important first step to unlocking the truths of Ecclesiastes: Your faith in God must be a dynamic, life-changing thing. Only by "tangling" with God can you ever hope to find eternal happiness, purpose and meaning.

Out of One Drink, into Another

I was a teenage alcoholic. Well, not really. Actually I was a Quikoholic—consumed by a burning desire to drown myself in gallons of Nestle's Quik chocolate milk.

I started young. Every day I would come home from the third grade and search the refrigerator for that necessary jug of milk. Then I would prepare the glass and spoon. When all was ready, carefully laid out and arranged on the gleaming Formica counter top, I would grab a kitchen stool, clamber to its top and regally open the doors to the cabinet—the one that held the Quik.

With bated breath and active slobber glands, I would firmly grasp the beloved can of Quik. Gently, so as not to disturb the crystalline contents, I would lower the object of my desires to the counter. Then, with a burst of speed because I could wait no more, I would spoon three heaping tablespoons (we Quikoholics can really take it) into the cup, pour in the milk (any idiot knows the Quik goes in first or it takes twice as long to mix out the lumps) and stir until the brew's consistency was perfectly smooth and creamy. I always used a clear glass so I could be sure to get all the chocolate mixed up off the bottom. (It is my considered opinion that the formula for Nestle's Quik has changed over the years. It used to be a lot harder to mix.)

It had to be Nestle's Quik chocolate. Nothing else would do. Heaven help my poor mother who, with great intentions and out of the goodness of her heart I am sure, one day brought home a can of strawberry–flavored Quik! Strawberry is for wimps, not for me. No, I had to have my daily after school Quik fix, or I was a nervous wreck with no meaning and purpose in life. I even put the stuff in my cereal.

Imagine my horror when, after an uncomfortably warm day in a crowded classroom, I came home to discover—terror of terrors—NO MILK! At first, I couldn't believe it. No milk? In desperation, the sweat running off my fevered brow, I threw the contents of the refrigerator's shelves to the floor. It was true. No milk. I panicked. "Think," I said to myself. "Think, think, think. Surely there must be some solution, some substitute for milk. There must be."

There wasn't. I tried the only thing we had available at the time: water. Have you ever mixed Quik with water? It doesn't really mix. It just turns into this muddy mess that looks like bits of dirt floating about. It's not quite a colloidal suspension, to use the scientific term.

Worse than that, it tastes terrible. Quik and water don't work.

The ultimate goal of the Christian life should be to grow as close to God as possible and to become as much like Him as we can. Each of us who claim the name of Christ as Lord should be "mixing" ourselves with our Lord—sort of like Quik is mixed with milk. When we dilute ourselves in the things of the world, we are like the foolish kid who tries to mix chocolate with tap water. Believe me, it's no substitute for the real thing.

All of this brings us to the heart of the book of Ecclesiastes. Solomon wanted to write a book about the meaning of life. In so doing, he wound up talking about the two most important things in the universe: God and people. God is most important of all because He made all! "Through him all things were made; without him nothing was made that has been made" (John 1:3). He is the center and source of everything, even if some tend to forget that. And each of us is important, of course. We're important to ourselves and to those who care for us.

The mixing of God and the individual is true living. So, when Solomon wrote about God and people, he came up with what amounts to a handbook about life.

Now, here's an important thing to understand about Ecclesiastes. As Solomon, who was reputed to be the world's wisest man, put his brain to work on the subject of the meaning of life, he quickly realized that, life is totally without meaning for a person who is separated from God.

What does this mean? It means that life without God doesn't add up to much.

In our study of Ecclesiastes, we will attempt to learn some important secrets of enjoying life as God intended. Just as milk and Nestle's Quik make a pretty good drink, we'll discover that God is the ingredient that can transform our lives from bland to great. The Bible will be our textbook, so be sure to have one in your lap as you read this book.

Meaning

Now let's take a look at the passage this chapter is based on, Ecclesiastes 1:1-11.

The Teacher is giving a lecture. And his thesis is that "everything is meaningless" (v. 2). As we'll see, Solomon was speaking as if he was completely without God in his life. It was not true, but for the sake of the point he was trying to make, he placed himself in the position of being a cynical, skeptical old man.

Beginning with verse 3, the cynical Teacher begins to elaborate on his idea that life is pointless. Here is a summary of verses 3-11:

If we work hard, we gain nothing. People die, the world still turns. Every day is the same—the sun goes around, the winds blow, the rivers flow. It's all boring. There's nothing new, everything is pointless. Nobody remembers you when you're gone.

Wow! Is this the kind of reality you want to live in? Probably not. In fact, it would be very difficult to find someone who behaved as if the Teacher was right. Even people who deny that God exists still feel that life has some ultimate value and purpose. To test this, let's try a little thought experiment.

Here is a list of bad things:

> Having sex before marriage.
> Spitting on the floor.
> Taking candy from babies.
> Gassing millions of innocent people in concentration camps.

Put the items in order of "badness" from bad to worse.

The list would have different arrangements in different cultures across the world. In some areas, spitting is perfectly all right. In other places, taking candy from a baby is not only not bad, it's considered the healthful thing to do. And, secular media in western cultures promotes rather than discourages sex before marriage.

The average person in any area of the world—whether atheist or religious would leave the fourth item at the bottom of the list. Why? Because wanton slaughter is a great wrong. It is a greater wrong than the others.

But if there is no meaning in life, then murder has no meaning. Therefore, it is not wrong.

Now our discussion has taken a strange twist. We could spend page after page arguing about the fact that if life had no meaning, then murder would not be wrong. But it really would be just a nonsense argument because the vast majority of people in all times and all places have felt strongly that murder is wrong. Even societies that condone murder, such as the fierce Yanamamo tribe in South America, only allow it under certain very strict conditions. There is something deep within each of us that denies the rightness of murder. Hitler is no sane person's hero.

Real people in the real world have a sense of right and wrong. Not only that, they have a sense that some things are "wronger" than others. But where did that sense come from? If life has no ultimate meaning, that sense would not exist. There would be no standard that would allow us to say that some things are only a little wrong and some things are very wrong. There would be no laws to forbid anything, because in a meaningless world laws would be meaningless. In fact, if life truly has no meaning, then we are just electrons and stuff floating around together until we die.

This is where God enters. He gives us our meaning. He created us and He placed within us, even within unbelievers, a sense that there is a standard by which we should live—a set of rules that say what is fair and what is unfair. In fact, this inner knowledge that there must be some purpose and meaning in life, some sense to the universe, is one of the major reasons people come to believe in God. And it's a very valid reason. Without a superior Creator, there couldn't possibly be meaning: Meaning can't evolve by itself.

Therefore, when the Teacher shouts, "Meaningless! Meaningless! Utterly meaningless! Everything is meaningless," he does so not so much with a sense of conviction but in a state of confusion. "Something's wrong," he seems to be saying. Of course something was wrong. The Teacher was speaking of the position of a man without God.

Our society is a society losing sight of God. It is therefore dangerously on the brink of becoming a society without meaning. And each individual who has lost sight of God is in the same quandary.

The solution is obvious: Find God.

Finding God

Now let's look at a man who serves as a perfect example of where most people find themselves on the road to a meaningful life. Turn to Mark 10:46-52 in your Bible, the story of a blind beggar named Bartimaeus.

Jericho was a very old town even in the time of Jesus. Because it had abundant water, it had been a stopping place for caravans and desert travelers for thousands of years.

Jericho had seen many powerful leaders come and go. But few would cause the stir caused by an itinerant preacher and healer known by the name of Jesus. His visit to the city was a major event. As He left, citizens crowded the roadside. Everybody was there to see the man some called the Lord and Son of God. They probably hoped Jesus would work a couple of juicy miracles so they would have something to tell their grandchildren. The festive, noisy crowd must have made quite a hubbub as each person tried to press in close to Jesus.

Off to the side of the dusty road sat a poor, blind beggar named Bartimaeus. Not much of a name. It means "Son of Timaeus." How would you like to be named something like "Daughter of Fred"?

If we use a bit of imagination, we can picture Bartimaeus dressed in tattered rags, picking the gaps between his brown teeth, holding out a battered cup, all the while muttering, "How about a handout?" He probably had a few goals in life: a new rag to wear during the chilly desert nights; perhaps a scrap of real meat for dinner; a fairly safe alley in which to sleep without fear of rowdies.

Into Bart's tiny world suddenly burst the clamor and confusion of the parade associated with Jesus' departure. "What's that?" the blind beggar shouted. "Hey! What's happening?"

Someone probably said, "Shut up, old man! It's Jesus!" With that Bartimaeus started screaming at the top of his lungs, "Jesus, Son of David, have mercy on me!" Maybe he swung his cane around, bashing people in the shins. Still he screamed, "Jesus, Son of David, have mercy on me!" (Mark 10:47).

Many gathered around him and told him to stuff a sock in it. He was an embarrassment. A sightless, useless tramp. "Shut up," the more rude members of the horde may have croaked. "Get out of here! You'll give Jericho a bad name."

Bartimaeus screeched all the more loudly, "JESUS, SON OF DAVID, HAVE MERCY ON ME!"

Jesus heard him, of course, and said, "Call him" (Mark 10:49).

So they called him, saying (with a rather quick change of attitude), "Cheer up! On your feet! He's calling you" (Mark 10:49). When the town's mayor saw this, he probably slapped himself on the forehead and thought, "Oh, no. All the city's dignitaries and leading citizens are here in our finest outfits and "jewels, and Jesus wants to talk to some burned out carcass who doesn't even pay taxes."

So Bartimaeus jumped up and came to the Lord. Jesus asked what at first seems to be a rather silly question: "What do you want me to do for you?" (Mark 10:51). But it wasn't silly. Bart may have wanted the latest model camel with the digital dashboard and electronic ignition. He may have wanted a new coat. He may even have wanted Jesus to yell at the crowd for being so mean to him. But Bart was no fool. He said, "I wanna SEEEEEEEEE!" (see v. 51).

Jesus admired the man's faith. After all, he had called Jesus the Son of David—a title reserved only for the Messiah. He was willing to look like a fool shouting for help and he believed that Jesus was the one to come to for help. In response to his faith, Jesus gave Bartimaeus sight. The man then followed Jesus along the road.

Bartimaeus is a perfect example of where most people find themselves on the road to a meaningful life. Most of us have little, tiny worlds in which we live. Our goals may be a bit bigger than a new rag to wear or a piece of meat to eat, but not much bigger. It's only when Jesus comes walking up our path that we can suddenly make the astonishing discovery of sight.

You see, Bartimaeus was out of it. He may have been told about light and color, but he had no real light and color in his life. He was missing an entire dimension. Only Jesus could give him this new dimension.

In the same way, anyone who is separated from God is in spiritual darkness. The dimension of meaning and purpose is gone. These people may fool themselves into thinking that a good job, a lofty education or a pretty spouse gives their lives real meaning, but they are mistaken. Even if these things did give meaning, what are they compared to living with Almighty God forever and ever? Our meaning comes only when we are connected with the giver of meaning. Only when we mix our lives with His do we truly have life. As Jesus so clearly said, "I have come that they may have life, and have it to the full" (John 10:10).

After each chapter in this book you will find questions and ideas to help you get a better understanding of how Ecclesiastes relates to your own life. If you are studying this book alone, you may wish to choose a few items to go over in detail. If you are studying this with other people, you can assign different items for each person or small group to study and discuss.

1. The eleventh chapter of Hebrews could be called "Faith's Hall of Fame" because it lists a great many people who had strong faith in God.

   Read Hebrews 11:13-16. How does the passage relate to meaning and purpose for a Christian?

   What is God not ashamed to be?

   What do you feel Mark Nakatsukasa's experience with the shark teaches you about the type of faith in God you should have?

2. Paul believed that the eternal things are the important things: "So we fix our eyes not on what is seen, but on what is unseen. For what is seen is temporary, but what is unseen is eternal" (2 Cor. 4:18).

   How does this idea of keeping our eyes on the eternal fit in with finding meaning here on earth?

3. Read John 15. There are many important thoughts in this chapter that relate to meaningfulness. List five of them.

4. The ultimate goal of the Christian life should be to grow as close to God as possible and to become as much like Him as we can. In addition to prayer and Bible study, list four or five other things you should be habitually practicing to become more like Him.

   What wonderful promise is made to us in 1 John 3:2?

   First John 3:3 contains one other thing you can add to your list from John 15.

5. Each of us who claims Christ as Lord should be mixing ourself

with our Lord—sort of like Nestle's Quik is mixed with milk. When we dilute ourselves in the things of the world, we are like the foolish kid who tries to mix the chocolate with tap water.

Give some examples of how a person can mix with God or dilute themselves in this world.

Here's a tough one: We all need possessions to keep us going in this world (clothes, car, food and so on), but how can we acquire these things without letting them become more important to us than God?

How can we know when we've begun to mess up?

6. Besides material possessions, what are some things that people tend to cling to in order to find meaning in life?

Which of these things are truly important in view of an eternity spent with or without Almighty God?

7. We have said that God is the center and source of everything. In other words, He's way bigger than the created universe. We use the prefix "omni", or "all." He is omnipotent (all-powerful), omnificent (unlimited in creative power), omniscient (all-knowing) and omnipresent (everywhere). If you would like to read some passages about these ideas, try Psalm 139, Psalm 147:5, and Matthew 19:23-26.

Just for fun, try the following challenge. God is bigger than the universe. Our Milky Way galaxy is, let's say, 100,000 light years across (it's actually quite a bit more than that). One light year is 6,000,000,000,000 (six trillion) miles. There are 5,280 feet in a mile. If everyone was six feet tall, how many people would it take to stretch across the Milky Way? God's BIG!

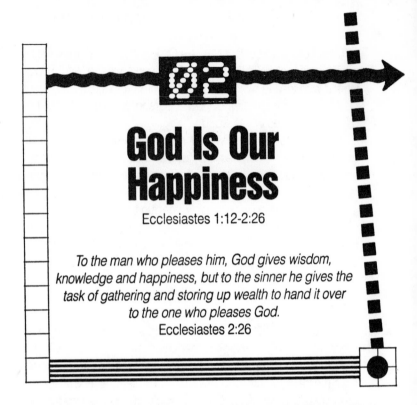

02

God Is Our Happiness

Ecclesiastes 1:12-2:26

*To the man who pleases him, God gives wisdom,
knowledge and happiness, but to the sinner he gives the
task of gathering and storing up wealth to hand it over
to the one who pleases God.*
Ecclesiastes 2:26

True happiness cannot be gained through human plans and efforts, but comes by acknowledging a powerful and loving God who gives us good gifts.

You may recall from your science classes that throughout history most people thought that the earth was the center of the universe. That's the way it seemed. Every day the sun came up, crossed the sky and went down. The stars marched across the sky at night.

Then along came a wise guy named Copernicus. He's the 15th century Polish astronomer who promoted the idea that the earth went around the sun. This made a lot of people mad, because it meant that they could no longer think of themselves as being at the center of God's creation. But eventually, everyone came to accept the idea that the sun was the center of the universe.

Just one problem with that—it's not true. Now we know that the sun travels through space, revolving around some point in our galaxy, in an orbit that takes about 250 billion years to complete. And if that isn't enough, the galaxy moves around some point in the local cluster of galaxies and *that* point travels though space toward some unknown source of gravity called the "Great Attractor." The center of the universe always seems to be somewhere else.

Life is a lot like that. We all try to center our lives on something of importance. When we are children, Mommy and Daddy are the center of our lives. But when we get a bit older, we realize that we can't base our lives on them any longer—the universe doesn't really revolve around them. It's time to move to a new center. That's when most people begin searching for life's answers. "What can I base my life on?" "What's really important?" "How can I find meaning?" "Where's my Nestle's Quik?" (Some of us are slower than others.)

And so the center begins to wander. The Teacher expresses pretty much the same idea in the passage from Ecclesiastes we are going to look at now. He realized that he needed to find something of value to center his life on. He hoped that in so doing, he would find meaning. He also realized that there was more than one thing he could center his life on. As we'll see when we read the passage (Eccles. 1:12-2:26), the Teacher tried three different centers before giving up. He tried *human wisdom, pleasure* and *achievement*.

Remember that in the first part of Ecclesiastes the Teacher had concluded that all is meaningless. Now, starting with 1:12, "Teach" shows how he arrived at that depressing evaluation.

In his attempt to find meaning, he conducted an experiment with his own life:

> *I, the Teacher, was king over Israel in Jerusalem. I devoted myself to study and to explore by wisdom all that is done under heaven. What a heavy burden God has laid on men! I have seen all the things that are done under the sun; all of*

them are meaningless, a chasing after the wind.
Ecclesiastes 1:12-14

Human Wisdom

I thought to myself, "Look, I have grown and increased in wisdom more than anyone who ruled over Jerusalem before me; I have experienced much of wisdom and knowledge." Then I applied myself to the understanding of wisdom, and also of madness and folly, but I learned that this, too, is a chasing after the wind.
For with much wisdom comes much
*   sorrow;*
* the more knowledge, the more*
*   grief.*
    Ecclesiastes 1:16-18

The wisdom the Teacher is looking at is human wisdom. He is looking at the world around him, the world without God.

Being the king of Israel, Solomon had the bucks and time it took to do a thorough job of researching the facts. First, he educated himself. Then he applied himself to the "understanding of wisdom, and also of madness and folly" (Eccles. 1:17). That is, he tried to be wise instead of an idiot. His conclusion? It was like trying to catch the wind. The more he learned, the more he realized he didn't really know.

Notice what the Teacher says in verse 13: "What a heavy burden God has laid on men!" This is the voice of frustration speaking. It's like saying, "Why did God make us if there is nothing of value to be gained?"

But then the Teacher made an even sadder discovery. In verse 18, he states that wisdom and knowledge bring sorrow and grief. Not only is human wisdom meaninglessness, it is *negative* meaninglessness. We live not just in a world with no point, we seemingly live in a world where people suffer for no good reason.

Have you ever seen real human suffering? It exists and it is rampant. Take a walk along any hospital corridor and peek in the doors. Old people dying of pneumonia. Young people with leukemia. Cancer victims in great pain, attached by tubes to the machines. This is in our rich, sophisticated society. In the poorer parts of the world, things are a lot worse.

I'll never forget the very first date I had with my then wife-to-be Brenda. I'll never forget it because it almost killed me! I was fine at the beginning of the date, but within a couple of hours I felt absolutely terrible. I drove myself home, shaking so badly I could barely steer. At home, I almost got stuck out in the cold: I could hardly get the key in the door lock because my hands were shaking so.

It wasn't love. It was double pneumonia. The doctor later told me that the drugs he used to help me had been on the market only for a few years. Before then, he said, it would have meant a "number six" body bag for me. Ulp!

During my stay in the hospital, I noticed a strange thing. All the nurses were spending a lot of time with me. There were at least a dozen other pneumonia patients on the floor, but the nurses all orbited around my bed, one or two at a time. I was hoping it was because of my great good looks, wit and charm—or perhaps my primitive animal magnetism. But no. It was, as one told me, because I was the only person under 75 in the pneumonia wing. I was the only one they could talk to! Everybody else was very old and the disease had made them all more or less crazy.

That was perhaps my first taste of the unfairness of life. I don't know who those old people were, but when they checked out of life they went out suffering. It didn't matter if they were rich, wise or powerful. This is just a minor example of the kind of thing the Teacher was struggling with. Life is unfair and he knew it.

So, disenchanted with knowledge and human wisdom, he tried the thing that all of us not-so-interested-in-education people can readily relate to: pleasure.

Pleasure

I thought in my heart, "Come now, I will test you with pleasure to find out what is good." But that also proved to be meaning-

less. "Laughter," I said, "is foolish. And what does pleasure accomplish?" Ecclesiastes 2:1,2

There is nothing necessarily wrong in pleasure and laughter, but the Teacher knew that they could not provide the central point to his life. If pleasure and laughter is all there is, then life is meaningless.

So guess what he tried next?

I tried cheering myself with wine, and embracing folly—my mind still guiding me with wisdom. I wanted to see what was worthwhile for men to do under heaven during the few days of their lives. Ecclesiastes 2:3

He became a party animal—King Spuds, I guess you could call him. It's not necessary to review the modern day accident statistics and the sad stories of too much to drink to try to find out what Solomon discovered. Read what he says in Proverbs 23:29-35:

Who has woe? Who has sorrow?
 Who has strife? Who has complaints?
 Who has needless bruises? Who has
   bloodshot eyes?
Those who linger over wine,
 who go to sample bowls of mixed
   wine.
Do not gaze at wine when it is red,
 when it sparkles in the cup,
 when it goes down smoothly!
In the end it bites like a snake
 and poisons like a viper.
Your eyes will see strange sights
 and your mind imagine confusing
   things.
You will be like one sleeping on the
   high seas,
 lying on top of the rigging.

> *"They hit me," you will say, "but I'm*
> *not hurt!*
> *They beat me, but I don't feel it!*
> *When will I wake up*
> *so I can find another drink?"*

That passage was written thousands of years ago, but it could have been said for the first time today. It could be describing overindulgence in the twentieth centur

Achievement

Returning to Ecclesiastes, we see in 2:4-10 that the Teacher, apparently having had his fill of wine and pleasure seeking, tries glorious achievements. He built houses and planted vineyards. He made gardens, parks and water systems. He acquired slaves. He amassed herds and flocks, silver and gold. He had singers to entertain him, and a harem as well. He achieved total greatness. He denied himself nothing at all—as king, he could take what he pleased.

The Teacher had it all—wisdom, pleasure and achievement. And this was no figment of Solomon's imagination. It was no exaggeration of the truth. Take a look at the kind of life Solomon led:

His wisdom: "God gave Solomon wisdom and very great insight, and a breadth of understanding as measureless as the sand on the seashore. Solomon's wisdom was greater than the wisdom of all the men of the East, and greater than all the wisdom of Egypt . . . . And his fame spread to all the surrounding nations. He spoke three thousand proverbs and his songs numbered a thousand and five . . . . Men of all nations came to listen to Solomon's wisdom, sent by all the kings of the world, who had heard of his wisdom" (1 Kings 4:29-34).

His pleasure: "The weight of the gold that Solomon received yearly was 666 talents" (1 Kings 10:14). "He had seven hundred wives of royal birth and three hundred concubines" (1 Kings 11:3).

That's about 25 tons of gold each year in today's measure, and 60 tons of women.

His achievement: For details of some of the incredibly ornate buildings he constructed, see 1 Kings 6—7 and 2 Chronicles 9:15-28.

> *Yet when I surveyed all that my hands*
> *had done*
> *and what I had toiled to achieve,*
> *everything was meaningless, a chasing*
> *after the wind;*
> *nothing was gained under the sun.*
> Ecclesiastes 2:11

So it comes down to this: Life centered on limited human understanding, pleasures or accomplishments just doesn't cut it.

It might be good to point out once again something we touched on lightly in the first chapter. Most of the people in this world attempt to find meaning in education, good jobs, relationships and so on. None of these things are particularly bad, but none of them provide *true* meaning. They can, however, provide a sort of counterfeit meaning. That is, people can fool themselves into thinking that they are living meaningful, purposeful lives.

The Teacher knew better. He looked at everything anyone could possibly do and realized that none of it meant much of anything. As we study the entire book of Ecclesiastes we will come to understand why he held that belief.

Perhaps it's time to take stock of our own lives. What do we find at the center?

One More Time
What did the Teacher do after he took stock of his life and concluded wisdom, pleasure and achievement are useless? He went back and explained his conclusion again.

Then I turned my thoughts to consider
    wisdom,
    and also madness and folly.
What more can the king's successor do
    than what has already been done?
I saw that wisdom is better than
    folly,
    just as light is better than darkness.
The wise man has eyes in his head,
    while the fool walks in darkness;
but I came to realize
    that the same fate overtakes them
        both.
Then I thought in my heart,
"The fate of the fool will overtake me
        also.
    What then do I gain by being
        wise?"
Ecclesiastes 2:12-15

The thrust of this passage is simple to understand. The Teacher tried it all. No successor could have tried more—certainly not us, since we don't have the fabulous wealth or opportunity to indulge ourselves that he did. And when he was finished trying it all, when he had thought it was better to be wise than foolish, he realized that in the end being wise had no value—the same fate awaits the wise and the foolish: death.

"So I hated life," the Teacher seems to shout (Eccles. 2:17). Yet still he carried on with his search. He returned to his experiment, trying achievement one more time.

In Ecclesiastes 2:17-23, the Teacher complained that all a person's accomplishments will end up in some successor's hands. "And who knows whether he will be a wise man or a fool?" (v. 19). In Solomon's case, everything he had went to a fool. After 40 years as supreme king in Israel, Solomon died and had to let go. His son Rehoboam took over. Within days, due to Rehoboam's unwise decision to reject the good advice of his father's counselors, the kingdom was split down the middle and the history of Israel was changed forever. (See 1 Kings 12 for details.)

Ecclesiastes 2:24,25 mark a departure from the "woe is me" dismal atmosphere of most of the Teacher's words:

> *A man can do nothing better than to eat and drink and find satisfaction in his work. This too, I see, is from the hand of God, for without him, who can eat or find enjoyment?*

The Teacher concluded that life centered on the things of this world leads to spiritual bankruptcy. God is the source of true and lasting enjoyment.

The Two Teachers

Jesus (who was often called Teacher) showed His agreement with the Teacher's discovery when He said:

> *"So do not worry, saying 'What shall we eat?' or 'What shall we drink?' or 'What shall we wear?' For the pagans run after all these things, and your heavenly Father knows that you need them. But seek first his kingdom and his righteousness and all these things will be given to you as well."* Matthew 6:31-33

This, then, is the meaning of life: Instead of centering yourself on the things of this world, center your life on the Creator of this world. God will then supply the things you wanted all along. Makes sense, doesn't it? God will give us the gifts we were created to enjoy—wisdom, pleasure, achievement and things like love and satisfaction—when we give ourselves fully to him.

It's kind of like basketball. One of the player positions on a basketball team is the center. I remember well the college basketball team I played on. I played the forward. I scored four points. (It's a good thing there wasn't a "threeward" position.) You probably think I'm kidding. Or maybe you think I only played a few minutes during one game. Sorry, no. I played almost every game of the two seasons I was on the squad. I scored four points. And I did better than two other guys!

As you can probably guess, it wasn't much of a team. We always got killed (except by the Pentecostal college guys across town). However, we had one guy on our team who was absolutely great. His name was Paul Brandon, feared far and wide for his incredible size and his reputation for no–holds–barred "jungle" ball. In other words, if you got in his way, he'd flatten you. Our team or their team, he'd flatten you. Too bad we didn't have a football team. Anyway, Paul was our center.

Now, the position is called center for a couple of reasons. One, the player stands more or less in the center of the action in front of the basket. But more importantly, the center *is* the center of action for many of the key plays. Much of what happens on the court depends on the center. The success of many plays, indeed, of the team, hinges on the ability of the center. That's why the tall guy goes there. To win at basketball you must center your team around the center.

When we look at what Jesus said in Matthew 6:31-33, we realize that He is simply telling us to center our lives on God. It has to be that way, for He is the source of everything that exists. He is therefore the source of human happiness, satisfaction and meaning.

Do you begin to see what's going on now? I don't mean do you just understand what Solomon was writing, but do you begin to understand what is happening in your life? If you are frustrated with the way things are going, it's probably because "things" are more important than God.

This is not an unusual condition, even for Christians. In fact, all Christians seem to have those days when the things of the world—good or bad—loom larger than their dependence on the Lord. But as we grow and mature, our perspective must change. Remember, the ultimate goal of each believer should be to grow as close to God and become as much like Him as possible. When we see things His way, we will stop seeing them in the negative, depressing way the Teacher did, and start understanding them the way Jesus—the real teacher—did.

Not all people will come to the wisdom of Jesus. For them, the Teacher has one more verse to look at:

To the man who pleases him, God gives wisdom, knowledge and happiness, but to the sinner he gives the task of gathering and storing up wealth to hand it over to the one who pleases God. This too is meaningless, a chasing after the wind. Ecclesiastes 2:26

This is an interesting statement. Notice the two ends of the spectrum of human desires: God gives wisdom, knowledge and happiness to the believer; the unbeliever gets the wealth, which is eventually lost to him or her. The Teacher then calls this meaningless.

It's meaningless until understood in the light of the teachings of Jesus. In Matthew 6:19-21 Jesus says, "Do not store up for yourselves treasures on earth, where moth and rust destroy, and where thieves break in and steal. But store up for yourselves treasures in heaven, where moth and rust do not destroy, and where thieves do not break in and steal. For where your treasure is, there your heart will be also."

This is what it boils down to: The complete, perfect fulfillment of life, the true revelation of meaningfulness, awaits us in heaven. Until that time, Christians can taste a bit of true life and meaningfulness here on earth. Nonbelievers can too, in a very limited sense, but they will lose it all in the end.

1. Here are some verses that expand some of the lessons taught in the Ecclesiastes passage you studied in this chapter: Psalm 127:2; Daniel 12:3; 1 Corinthians 2:6-16; 10:31; Revelation 14:13.

   Read these passages and see if you can match them to appropriate parts of Ecclesiastes 1:12-2:26.

   How does the wisdom of 1 Corinthians 2:6-16 differ from the Teacher's wisdom?

2. Mom and Dad are the centers of most little kids' lives. What are

some of the things that people your age tend to center their lives on?

What do you think is the center of your own life right now?

3. How do you define happiness?

What makes you happy?

Do you think God's definition of happiness is different from your own?

4. Why do you think there is suffering? That's a question that has confused a lot of people through the centuries! Read Ecclesiastes 1:13.

Do you suppose God allows suffering (allows, not causes—Adam and Eve's sin of rejecting God's rule is the real source of suffering) in order to communicate an important message to humanity?

If so, what is the message?

5. In Ecclesiastes 2:14-16 the Teacher bemoans his fate. What difference is there between the fate of the fool and the wise?

If the Teacher had been speaking from a Christian's view of death and eternal life, how do you think his statement would have changed?

6. Have you ever hated life (see Eccles. 2:17)? Do you know anyone who seems to hate life?

What, for people your age, are some of the common causes of this sense of frustration?

What could you tell someone to help him or her understand the solution?

7. Here is a well-known mathematical equation: $2 + 2 = 4$. Using the truths discussed in this chapter, create a formula that adds up to a meaningful life.

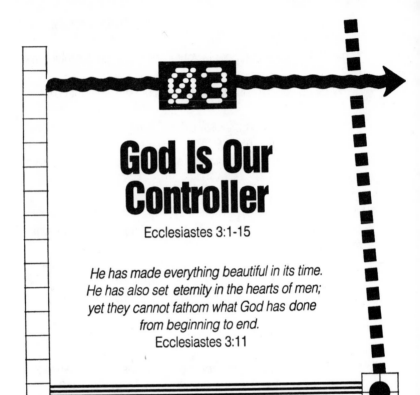

03

God Is Our Controller

Ecclesiastes 3:1-15

*He has made everything beautiful in its time.
He has also set eternity in the hearts of men;
yet they cannot fathom what God has done
from beginning to end.*
Ecclesiastes 3:11

God is in control of everything that happens in this world, but as finite humans we will often have to accept and trust that control without understanding what God is doing.

et's try a little experiment. Find a nice, large crowd of people and get in the middle of it. A shopping mall or school classroom would be excellent for our purposes. Now, without warning, scream at the top of your lungs, "OGG HOGGA BOOM DE BOOM! KREE GORGO WATA HEY!" At the same time, run and jump and tear out your hair. Do this until the men in the white suits come and take you away.

Your experiment has proved an important law of human nature: People like control. They don't like chaos. That's why if you carry out the experiment described in the previous paragraph, you'd find yourself moldering in a rubber room down at the mental hospital.

The Teacher takes up the subject of control in Ecclesiastes 3:1-15. In verse 1, he says, "There is a time for everything, and a season for every activity under heaven." Then he goes on to tell us that there are times to be born, die, plant, uproot, kill, heal, tear down, build, weep, laugh, mourn, dance, scatter, gather, embrace, refrain from embracing, search, give up searching, keep, throw away, tear, mend, be silent, speak up, love, hate, make war and make peace.

Here is the problem: We want to control our lives, but it's impossible—it can't be done. There are far too many decisions to make and we do not have enough insight. How can anyone realistically expect to always know the right times to do all the things the Teacher listed? Even if we know the right time to laugh, for example, soon something would come along to make us cry—there are so many circumstances beyond our control.

A realistic non-Christian must look at this passage with a great deal of gloom. If there is no God to control these things, then life is just a series of "stabs in the dark"—trying to do the right things while having very little knowledge and control of the situation. Life with no God would be controlled by the whims of circumstance. It would be chaos.

A Christian can look at it differently. We understand that God ultimately is in control of all these things. This should give us a great deal of joy. God is in charge. Although with our very limited vision we cannot see or understand all the various aspects of life, we know that God can. He orders our lives for us. Romans 8:28 says, "And we know that in all things God works for the good of those who love him, who have been called according to his purpose."

The Road to Emmaus

A classic example of God's control is found in Luke 24:13-35, the story of two disciples leaving town just after Jesus was crucified.

As it happened, the two disciples were traveling away from the terrible scene of the Crucifixion. They had just lost their Lord, they saw His death and they undoubtedly were leaving with a tremendous sense of frustration and failure. The ride was over. Jesus had lost. Everything they had hoped for was at an end. Life had spun out of control.

Verses 15 and 16 tell us, "As they talked and discussed these things with each other, Jesus himself came up and walked along with them; but they were kept from recognizing him."

The resurrected Lord asked them what they were talking about. They spilled it out in a mixture of confusion and disappointment.

Jesus replied, in verse 25: "How foolish you are, and how slow of heart to believe all that the prophets have spoken! Did not the Christ have to suffer these things and then enter his glory?" Then He explained to them what the Old Testament said concerning Himself.

Later that day, when the two disciples finally realized who they had been listening to, they joyfully sped back to Jerusalem to tell the rest of the gang what had happened. They probably covered the seven or eight miles in three leaps.

But they were a bit late—when they got there, the other disciples were already buzzing about Peter, who had also seen Jesus. If that wasn't enough, just then "Jesus himself stood among them and said to them, 'Peace be with you'" (v. 36).

The disciples learned in a very graphic way that even when things seem completely dismal, God has not lost control. He is in charge at all times. He can and does step into our lives. We may be slow to see Him, but He is there. He can miraculously deal with any problem we face—not always the moment we hope He would, but when He in His wisdom thinks best.

The problem is not that God is not in control of our lives. The problem is, as Jesus said, we are foolish and slow to believe it.

But What Sort of Control?
There is a shopping center in my neighborhood on the island of Kauai that sponsors fun events like customized truck shows, free refreshments and crab races. Yes, that's right: crab races.

Crab races are great. The racetrack is a ramp about twenty feet long. The crabs, collected down at the beach and numbered with a felt pen, are dumped out of a box at the top of the ramp. The first crab to scoot down the ramp and cross the finish line is the winner. Those crabs can really move! Most races last three or four seconds. The people who race really get into it, shouting and yelling and trying to scare their crabs down the ramp. The winning crab from each race moves up to the final rounds.

Is this the sort of control God exercises over us? Is He some kind of "crab racer" who dumps us onto the racetrack of life for His own entertainment? Do we sweat and dash madly toward the finish line, some to be winners and some to be losers?

No. God has given us a lot of responsibility in life. He allows us to make choices and decisions. Though we are ultimately in His control, He in turn expects us to act wisely and live according to high standards of behavior. The Bible is full of rules to live by. They wouldn't be there if God exercised total and complete control on every move we make. We are not machines. God gave us brains.

Now and then a crab will jump over the low rail of the ramp and zoom away across the parking lot. Along comes a car and—splat!—no more crab. The crab broke the rules, he went out of bounds and paid the price for it. The Bible tells us about the limits that God has set for us. We can choose to live by His rules or we can choose to perish without them.

The Teacher understood this principle. "I know that there is nothing better for men than to be happy and to do good while they live" (Eccles. 3:12). The Teacher realized that God expects His people to act wisely and righteously. This is an extremely important lesson to remember!

Anybody who has been in charge of a youth group for any time at all has seen the "wayward crab syndrome." In perhaps every group of young Christians, there are those who want to test the limits. Instead of staying away from wrong things, they want to get as close as they can without being burned.

In his book, *The Youth Worker's Book of Case Studies,* Jim Burns quotes a 17-year-old who is talking to a youth minister about her problem:

Bob and I went "all the way" once. That month I missed my period but I didn't think much about it. The next month I missed my period and went to a doctor. I am pregnant. I told Bob. He gave me $100 for an abortion and told me that he is transferring away from the area and never wants to see me again. I don't want to tell my family. And I don't want to carry a baby and be a disgrace to all I've stood for. If I keep the baby I'll ruin my chances for going to law school.[1]

All the way just once, and look how it turned out. It's sad she can't go back and live the way God advised in the Bible. She thought she was in control and she learned differently. The girl would probably love for God to step in and take miraculous control now. To somehow delete the life inside her or to turn back the clock so she can stay home alone watching TV rather than head out with Bob on that fateful day.

Yes, God is in ultimate control. But He has allowed us room to move. If we choose to move toward Him, we will win. If we choose to move away from Him, we will lose.

Beautiful Control

What does the worker gain from his toil? I have seen the burden God has laid on men. He has made everything beautiful in its time. He has also set eternity in the hearts of men; yet they cannot fathom what God has done from beginning to end. Ecclesiastes 3:9-11

The Teacher returns to the idea of Ecclesiastes 1:3: "What does man gain from all his labor at which he toils under the sun?" If God is not in control, then what the Teacher is saying is right—all is a waste of time. But the Teacher doesn't stop there. He says, "[God] has made everything beautiful in its time" (Eccles. 3:11). The word "beautiful" means, in this case, "appropriate." That is, God has made everything appropriate for its time. It all fits together like the pieces of a puzzle.

This concept that everything fits and makes sense would have given the Old Testament patriarch Abraham some problems. God told Abraham, "Take your son, your only son Isaac, whom you love, and go to the region of Moriah. Sacrifice him there as a burnt offering on one of the mountains I will tell you about" (Gen. 22:2). Can you imagine what a shocker that must have been? We all wonder what it would be like if God suddenly appeared in a vision and spoke to us. Can you imagine—God finally appears to you, just you, and what is His wonderful message? Set your kid on fire.

Of course we know that God had no intention of harming Isaac. But at the time Abraham must have believed he was really supposed to offer his son as a human sacrifice. The worshipers of pagan gods in the area offered human sacrifices all the time. At that point in his life, Abraham had no idea that the true God was any different.

What were Abraham's inner thoughts as he walked the long road to the altar with his child? If he could have looked forward in time and read the words of Ecclesiastes 3:11—"He has made everything beautiful in its time"—he probably would have said, "Oh, really?"

And what about the many hurting people that Jesus healed? The lepers, the lame, the blind—before they met Jesus, would they have found comfort in the words that "God has made everything beautiful in its time"? Not likely.

How many people today really believe that "In all things God works for the good of those who love him, who have been called according to his purpose" (Rom. 8:28)? Terrible things happen. Parents get divorced, accidents maim and kill, alcoholism wrecks families, young girls get pregnant. How can these things really be "beautiful"?

There is a key to understanding how bad things can be beautiful. The key is this: Bad things become beautiful when God steps in.

In Abraham's case, God was involved from beginning to to end. At the right moment He revealed His purpose to Abraham:

"Do not lay a hand on the boy . . . . Do not do anything to him. Now I know that you fear God, because you have not withheld

from me your son, your only son .... I swear by myself, declares the Lord, that because you have done this and have not withheld your son, your only son, I will surely bless you and make your descendants as numerous as the stars in the sky and as the sand on the seashore. Your descendants will take possession of the cities of their enemies, and through your offspring all nations on earth will be blessed, because you have obeyed me." Genesis 22:12,16-18

God kept His promise. Abraham's descendants are the Jews, and the offspring through whom all nations have been blessed is Jesus Christ. A bad thing became beautiful.

And what about sick people? Jesus stepped in and made sick people whole. When He touched them, life became beautiful. In every case in the Bible, when God steps in, He makes things right.

And He still does that today. There is nothing beautiful or even appropriate about divorce. But God can step in and heal the hearts of those who have been so hurt. People hurt in accidents, families torn apart by alcoholism, girls with unwanted pregnancies—all these things are sad and terrible. But none of it is beyond God's ability to step in and put things in order.

Yet it is so hard for us to see how He can do it. In our heads, we know that God can help us in whatever situation life has placed us. But our hearts are slow to believe.

The Teacher understood how difficult it is for us to see how God can make our lives beautiful. In the last part of verse 11, the Teacher says that God "has also set eternity in the hearts of men; yet they cannot fathom what God has done from beginning to end." In other words, there is something inside each of us that says, "There is more to life than this! There must be some reason and purpose for what is happening to me." The natural person suspects there's something more to life than the day-to-day grind or the tragedies, but it's hard to know what that something is.

A Dilemma

There is a dilemma found in Ecclesiastes 3:11. God has placed in order every happening in our world: "He has made everything beautiful in its time." Furthermore, he has given us a sense that life should be something grand: "He has also set eternity in the hearts of men." But complete understanding eludes us: "Yet they cannot fathom what God has done from beginning to end."

We all want to know the reason things happen as they do. We all wish we could make the important decisions in life with accuracy and foresight. But no matter how hard we try, we can't. God knows exactly what He's doing and He is in control of this planet. But we don't always know what He's doing. This is "the burden God has laid on men" (v. 10).

If God is in control, and we really can't know what He is doing or going to do, what should our response be? Abraham again serves as an example from which we can learn an important truth:

> *By faith Abraham, when God tested him, offered Isaac as a sacrifice. He who had received the promises was about to sacrifice his one and only son, even though God had said to him, "It is through Isaac that your offspring will be reckoned." Abraham reasoned that God could raise the dead, and figuratively speaking, he did receive Isaac back from death.*
> Hebrews 11:17-19

Abraham had faith that God knew what He was doing. He believed it so much that he was willing, at God's command, to slay the son through whom a whole nation of people was to come. A dead son can't raise a nation! But Abraham believed in God's promises.

Faith and obedience are the responses we must have. God is in ultimate control. As long as we stick close to Him, things will eventually turn out beautiful.

Question: How can a Christian believe God is in control when he or she is sticking as close to God as possible, yet still Mom is leaving Dad, Older Brother is on drugs, Little Sister has leukemia and Dad abuses them all? How can we turn to God in faith when deep inside we know that our parents are going to split, Big Brother is going to jail, Little Sister is going to die and Dad is not going to stop?

Once again the life of Abraham has something to say to us:

> *By faith Abraham, when called to go to a place he would later receive as his inheritance, obeyed and went, even though he did not know where he was going. By faith he made his home in the promised land like a stranger in a foreign country; he lived in tents, as did Isaac and Jacob, who were heirs with him of the same promise. For he was looking forward to the city with foundations, whose architect and builder is God.*
>
> *All these people [Old Testament heroes of faith] were still living by faith when they died. They did not receive the things promised; they only saw them and welcomed them from a distance .... Instead, they were longing for a better country—a heavenly one.* Hebrews 11:8-10,13,16

Isn't that incredible? They died without the promises. But by faith they knew that God would fulfill His commitment in heaven.

Some things will be seen by us to be beautiful only when we have the knowledge and understanding we'll receive in heaven. I don't know why people suffer. No one can explain how a plane full of people going down can be reconciled with God's control. Where do divorce, substance abuse, fatal illnesses and family violence fit into the scheme of things? These questions will only be answered in our future home. But they will be answered. Our responsibility right now is to trust God's wisdom and to give our lives in obedience to Him. By faith I know that God hates these terrible things we've been talking about. He is not the cause of them. But how it all fits together I cannot now comprehend.

We have eternity in our hearts. We were made for eternity. All dreams will come true there, not here.

Taking Advantage

Let's review what we've learned so far: We want to control our lives, but we aren't wise enough; God is in control; God allows us to make choices and decisions, even poor ones; God "works for the good of those who love him, who have been called according to his pur-pose" (Rom. 8:28); bad things become beautiful when God steps in; we are foolish and slow to believe these things; our responsibility is to trust God's wisdom and to give our lives to Him.

Logically, then, this is what we should do: We should seek to live under God's control rather than our own, we should base our choices and decisions on His wisdom (the Bible), we should love Him, we should be seeking God's presence (wanting Him to "step in") in both the good and the bad times, we must learn to have faith and we must trust God and give our lives fully to Him. This exactly describes the experience of living and growing as a Christian.

What tremendous power we Christians have! And what a fantas-tic future. God never guarantees to remove all problems for us in this life, but we know that He is in control and that He has prepared a place for us in heaven.

But how many Christians really live as if they believe God is in charge? If God is truly God, and if we are related to Him by way of the salvation that Jesus gives, then we should take advantage of these things. That is, we should rejoice and enjoy life. It's a gift. All things good and bad are somehow mixed together in God's plan. And we are right there in the middle of His plan. I don't want to be sitting on the sideline chewing my fingernails.

The Gift of God
The Teacher concludes this portion of Ecclesiastes with:

> *I know that there is nothing better for men than to be happy and do good while they live. That everyone may eat and drink, and find satisfaction in all his toil—this is the gift of God. I know that everything God does will endure forever; nothing can be added to it and nothing taken from it. God does it so that men may revere him.*
> *Whatever is has already been,*
> *and what will be has been before;*
> *and God will call the past to account.*
>   Ecclesiastes 3:12-15

Once again we come to the main theme of Ecclesiastes: Life not centered on God is meaningless. No one can control what life presents. Some will get lucky and have a nice life—they will eat and drink and find satisfaction. Others will have to suffer poverty or pain. God allows these things to happen so that people will revere Him. From a worldly viewpoint that's about all there is to life. Life on earth is all there is.

But we know better, don't we?

1. Remember our little experiment at the beginning of the chapter? If you yelled, "OGG HOGGA BOOM DE BOOM! KREE GORGO WATA HEY!" and ran and jumped and tore out your hair, you'd eventually be locked up. The experiment demonstrated that people like control. They don't like chaos. There seem to be exceptions to every rule, however. What would happen if you yelled, "OGG HOGGA BOOM DE BOOM! KREE GORGO WATA HEY!" and ran and jumped and tore out your hair at a Chicago Bears football game? Nothing! They would think you were just another fan. Football games are good examples of control in action. To someone who doesn't know the rules, football seems like chaos. But we know that the game, the teams and each play and player are carefully controlled. In fact, there are even rules of behavior imposed on the fans in the stands. Acting crazy is OK only up to certain point. You can dress weird and act weird, but you can't throw other fans from the roof of the stadium.

   Can you think of some ways the referees, rules, penalties, players, plays, injuries, goals, fans and other things associated with a football game can be viewed as allegories for God, life, making decisions, control, faith in God's control and so on? Match elements from the game with elements from life.

2. The Teacher says that there is a time for everything, and then gives a sample list in Ecclesiastes 3:1-8. Look at the list and see if you can identify times when the things listed are appropriate or not appropriate. For instance, are hate and war ever appropriate and if so, when?

Why are human beings not so good at knowing when to do or when to avoid all these things?

3. Romans 8:28 says, "And we know that in all things God works for the good of those who love him, who have been called according to his purpose." What is the promise made in this verse?

What are the conditions that must be met?

What does it mean to love God—that is, what are some things a person who loves God would do to demonstrate his or her love?

What does it mean to be called according to God's purpose?

Do you think God has called you for some purpose?

4. In Luke 24:25, Jesus told the two disciples who were leaving the scene of the crucifixion, "How foolish you are, and how slow of heart to believe all that the prophets have spoken! Did not the Christ have to suffer these things and then enter his glory?" Then Jesus explained to them what the Old Testament said concerning Himself. The reasons behind Christ's death were found in the words of the prophets, which Jesus explained to the disciples using the Old Testament. How can Bible study help a person understand why things good and bad happen in life?

How well do you think a person should know the Bible?

How often should a Christian read the Bible?

What happens to the Christian who evades Bible study?

5. If God wants to be in control, why did He give the angels and humanity decision-making power? Rebellion was the result both in heaven and on earth. What provisions did God make to heal the wounds of rebellion?

What must a person do to get right with God?

How can a Christian keep making the sort of choices that please God?

6. Have there been times in your life that didn't seem "beautiful"? (see Eccles. 3:11.)

What were some of those times?

Did God eventually show you how any of them fit into the puzzle of His will? If not, when do you think you will understand why those things happened?

Is it possible that some of the things happened because of your own bad choices? If so, how can you avoid making these same sort of mistakes in the future?

Sometimes bad things happen that we have no control over at all. What are some typical examples?

Could making certain positive decisions help a person cut down on the possibility of things going wrong? Give some examples.

7. We said that our responsibility is to trust God's wisdom and to give our lives to Him. How can these things provide meaning to life?

Note

1. Jim Burns, *The Youth Worker's Book of Case Studies* (Ventura: Gospel Light Publications, 1987) p. 12.

God Is Our Comforter

Ecclesiastes 3:16—4:16

*Again I looked and saw all the oppression
that was taking place under the sun:
I saw the tears of the oppressed—
and they have no comforter;
power was on the side of their oppressors—
and they have no comforter.*
Ecclesiastes 4:1

Injustice will always exist in this world. Christians should hate injustice and do what they can to ease suffering caused by it.

By this time the general message of Ecclesiastes is pretty clear: People fail miserably when they try to make sense of life on their own through various pursuits "under the sun." (The phrase "under the sun" is a signal that the Teacher is speaking from a worldly position.) Occasionally the Teacher offers an alternative to the hopeless efforts of people by suggesting that they put their trust in God and enjoy His good gifts. But, in general, he has built a case to prove that even the most successful life in a human sense, is a failure if it is lived apart from God. And now, in the passage we are about to examine, the Teacher draws our attention to what is perhaps the ultimate example of human failure—injustice.

The sorry way people sometimes treat each other shows how far sin has polluted human nature. Sin twists and perverts. It kills. "The wages of sin is death" (Rom. 6:23). But it is death that begins before the grave. Spiritual death can occur long before the body stops functioning.

The evidence of physical death is a body in the ground. The evidence of spiritual death is our poor, ungodly behavior. The injustice we see so much of in the world is evidence of spiritual deadness.

Injustice in Human Affairs

And I saw something else under the sun:
In the place of judgment—wickedness
was there,
in the place of justice—wickedness
was there.
Ecclesiastes 3:16

What the Teacher saw is this: Even those institutions which have been specifically set up to enforce justice and humane behavior are corrupt and evil! The legislative systems, courts, police forces and welfare systems have all missed the mark. (The very existence of these institutions prove that people are not naturally kind to each other.) Injustice extends all the way up to the oppressive acts of evil governments and all the way down to the unkindnesses that little kids can show each other. We can read about injustice in the newspaper headlines of wars and terrorism and we can experience it ourselves almost daily in unfair or unkind acts at home, in school or on the job.

There are two possible responses to injustice: (1) We can become desensitized to injustice. We can stop caring. (2) We can fight for what is right and fair. We can get involved.

Do not fool yourself into thinking you hate injustice—not if you don't try to do anything about it. To ignore another person's dilemma is just as unjust as causing it. If you cheat on a test, you are hurting the students who studied hard for that test—an injustice. But if you know someone who cheated and do nothing to set things right, you are also unjust.

On the other hand, you may be the type of person who wants to set things right. Perhaps you are involved in some sort of volunteer work at church or through a charitable organization. Great! But here's the bad news. If you have been involved, you know how impossible it is for one person—or even a huge organization—to really change the way this world operates.

The Teacher knew all of this. His response was: "I thought in my heart, 'God will bring to judgment both the righteous and the wicked, for there will be a time for every activity, a time for every deed'" (Eccles. 3:17). He knew that only God is able to bring true justice. You see, God has the two things necessary to make everything right. He has total and complete knowledge of what's going on down here and He has the infinite power to change things. Someday, God will judge each and every person. The apostle John wrote about this in Revelation 20:11-15:

Then I saw a great white throne and him who was seated on it. Earth and sky fled from his presence, and there was no place for them. And I saw the dead, great and small, standing before the throne, and books were opened. Another book was opened, which is the book of life. The dead were judged according to what they had done as recorded in the books. The sea gave up the dead that were in it, and death and Hades gave up the dead that were in them, and each person was judged according to what he had done. Then death and Hades were thrown into the lake of fire. The lake of fire is the second death. If anyone's name was not found written in the book of life, he was thrown into the lake of fire.

In Matthew 25:31-46 Jesus spoke of how He would judge the righteous and the unrighteous:

"When the Son of Man comes in his glory, and all the angels with him, he will sit on his throne in heavenly glory. All the nations will be gathered before him, and he will separate the people one from another as a shepherd separates the sheep from the goats. He will put the sheep on his right and the goats on his left.

"Then the King will say to those on his right, 'Come, you who are blessed by my Father; take your inheritance, the kingdom prepared for you since the creation of the world. For I was hungry and you gave me something to eat, I was thirsty and you gave me something to drink, I was a stranger and you invited me in, I needed clothes and you clothed me, I was sick and you looked after me, I was in prison and you came to visit me.'

"Then the righteous will answer him, 'Lord, when did we see you hungry and feed you, or thirsty and give you something to drink? When did we see you a stranger and invite you in, or needing clothes and clothe you? When did we see you sick or in prison and go to visit you?'

"The King will reply, 'I tell you the truth, whatever you did for the least of these brothers of mine, you did for me.'

"Then he will say to those on his left, 'Depart from me, you who are cursed, into the eternal fire prepared for the devil and his angels. For I was hungry and you gave me nothing to eat, I was thirsty and you gave me nothing to drink, I was a stranger and you did not invite me in, I needed clothes and you did not clothe me, I was sick and in prison and you did not look after me.'

"They also will answer, 'Lord, when did we see you hungry or thirsty or a stranger or needing clothes or sick or in prison, and did not help you?'

"He will reply, 'I tell you the truth, whatever you did not do for one of the least of these, you did not do for me.'

"Then they will go away to eternal punishment, but the righteous to eternal life."

God's judgment will be swift and final—and accurate. No one will be able to stand up and say, "Hey, wait a minute! I've been ripped off!" There will be no higher court of appeal, for there will be no need for appeal. God's judgment will be justice in action. Happily, for those who have thrown themselves on the mercy of the court (by becoming Christians), there is mercy: "Therefore, there is now no condemnation for those who are in Christ Jesus, because through Christ Jesus the law of the Spirit of life set me free from the law of sin and death" (Rom. 8:1,2). God's justice is always tempered with mercy. Christians deserve wrath just like everyone else, but Jesus suffered it for us on the cross.

Because God is in ultimate control and will bring justice to the unjust, we should follow these words from Romans 12:17-21:

> *Do not repay anyone evil for evil. Be careful to do what is right in the eyes of everybody. If it is possible, as far as it depends on you, live at peace with everyone. Do not take revenge, my friends, but leave room for God's wrath, for it is written: "It is mine to avenge; I will repay," says the Lord. On the contrary:*
> *"If your enemy is hungry, feed him;*
> *if he is thirsty, give him something to drink.*
> *In doing this, you will heap burning coals on his head."*
> *Do not be overcome by evil, but overcome evil with good.*

The Animals

Because God's judgment was still far in the future, the Teacher expressed a great sense of frustration. Desiring to find an answer that could be applied not in the far future but in the present, he came up with an interesting but imperfect solution to man's inhumanity to man. Before we get to that part, however, let's take a look at a comparison the Teacher draws between man and animals:

> *I also thought, "As for men, God tests them so that they may see that they are like the animals. Man's fate is like that of the*

animals; the same fate awaits them both: As one dies, so dies the other. All have the same breath; man has no advantage over the animal. Everything is meaningless. All go to the same place; all come from dust, and to dust all return. Who knows if the spirit of man rises upward and if the spirit of the animal goes down into the earth?" Ecclesiastes 3:18-21

Wow! At this point the Teacher says there is no difference between people and cockroaches. We all die and crumble into dust. If there is no God and no resurrection from the dead, this would be right. For those people who have no faith and therefore no hope, this passage must seem distressingly accurate.

But there is a God and there is resurrection from death:

This grace was given us in Christ Jesus before the beginning of time, but it has now been revealed through the appearing of our Savior, Christ Jesus, who has destroyed death and has brought life and immortality to light through the gospel.
2 Timothy 1:9,10

Notice that this passage answers the Teacher's question about knowing if we go "upward" after death. We now know and can place our confidence in the fact that we will all continue on after physical death—we know because Jesus said so.

"So I saw that there is nothing better for a man than to enjoy his work, because that is his lot. For who can bring him to see what will happen after him?" (Eccles. 3:22). Jesus can bring us to see what will happen, and the discovering of what awaits us in heaven is a great pleasure and joy.

Examples of Injustice

Again I looked and saw all the oppression that was taking place under the sun:
I saw the tears of the oppressed—
*   and they have no comforter;*
power was on the side of their oppressors—

and they have no comforter.
Ecclesiastes 4:1

The powerful were—and still are—oppressing the weak. The teacher was heartsick over this situation, which was made all the worse because "they have no comforter." Once again Jesus provides an entirely different point of view:

"And I will ask the Father, and He will give you another Helper, that He may be with you forever;
that is the Spirit of truth, whom the world cannot receive, because it does not behold Him or know Him, but you know Him because He abides with you, and will be in you."
John 14:16,17, *NASB*

The word "Helper" can also be thought of as "comforter." In the midst of injustice, our comfort comes from God by way of the Holy Spirit who lives in us. The disciples to whom Jesus made His promise would many times experience the Spirit's comforting touch while they suffered persecution and imprisonment. Stephen, the very first Christian to die for his faith, was "full of the Holy Spirit" at the time of his death (see Acts 7:54-60). This same Spirit still comforts us today, even if our troubles are minor.

The Teacher, however, lived many hundreds of years before Jesus promised to send the Helper. He was so upset by the injustice he saw in a world estranged from God that he declared that it was better to never have been born at all (see Eccles. 4:2,3). Perhaps this same attitude fills the hearts of those poor people who attempt to take their own lives. In a recent survey, 46 percent of the high school students interviewed said they know someone who has committed or attempted suicide. Over 30 percent said they considered suicide themselves, including 4 percent who actually tried to kill themselves. The sad result is that suicide has become the third major cause of death for teenagers.[1] In some age groups in some areas, suicide is now the number one cause of death. There is a deep need for Christian teenagers to tell their peers that there is hope. The pain and injustice of this world will one day end. And Jesus has promised to be with His followers during all their troubles (see Matt. 28:20b). But Jesus does not want us to retreat from the world to the safety of our relationship with Him. He wants us to bring His love to a hurting world. To do this we must become aware of the problems we're dealing with. The Teacher of Ecclesiastes lays the problems on the line one by one.

In Ecclesiastes 4:4, the Teacher broadens the scope of his indictment. He had condemned the powerful as oppressors of the weak, but now he concludes that all humans great and small are responsible for injustice: "And I saw that all labor and all achievement spring from man's envy of his neighbor. This too is meaningless, a chasing after the wind." In our drive to get ahead, we are pitted one against the other.

But the Teacher does not want his listeners to conclude that the answer to this dilemma is to be found in total passivity (the doormat syndrome). He says, "The fool folds his hands and ruins himself" (v. 5). The solution, according to the Teacher, is to share and share alike. "Better one handful with tranquility than two handfuls with toil and chasing after the wind" (v. 6). In the thousands of years since he wrote his statement, human history has proven the futility of the Teacher's wisdom. He's right, but nobody listens.

Companionship

In verses 7 and 8, the Teacher begins to lead into his interesting but not quite perfect solution to man's inhumanity to man, the solution that he hoped could be applied not in the far future but in the day-to-day lives of everyday people.

He describes "a man all alone" who works endlessly, never content with the riches he has amassed. He has no time for other things—no family or friends. Finally he realizes the damage his competitive drive has done. He has no one and no joy. "This too is meaningless—a miserable business!" (v. 8).

Now the Teacher suggests a way to choke off the despair of meaninglessness and to find a bit of joy and purpose: companionship.

Two are better than one,
because they have a good return for
their work:
If one falls down,
his friend can help him up.
But pity the man who falls
and has no one to help him up!
Also, if two lie down together, they will
keep warm.
But how can one keep warm alone?
Though one may be overpowered,
two can defend themselves.
A cord of three strands is not quickly
broken.
Ecclesiastes 4:9-12

We see here a journey through life. A person alone on the road will tend to stumble and fall, become cold and be overpowered by bandits. But there is safety in numbers. A person with friends has a better chance.

The imagery in this passage is figurative. The stumbling and falling likely refer to errors of judgment and to sins. A good friend will help steer his or her pal onto the right path. The coldness alluded to in the passage probably refers to the coldness of our world, the injustice we find all about us.

The highway robbers also alluded to perhaps speak of the attacks of the devil or the unpleasant circumstances that come without warning. The last sentence, "A cord of three strands is not quickly broken," may be suggesting that oppressed people can find comfort in mutual support.

The Teacher has hit upon the best solution the world has to offer to the pains of this world. For the people on this planet who will never experience the liberation and fulfillment of eternal life with God in heaven, good companionship is the best thing that will ever happen. Good friends, whether family members or spouses or outside acquaintances, are a gift from God that is available to all. Yes, the world is filled with suffering. Yes, life is sometimes tough. But friends help. A problem shared is a problem halved.

This lends added impact to the statement Jesus made when He told His disciples, "You are my friends if you do what I command. I no longer call you servants, because a servant does not know his master's business. Instead, I have called you friends, for everything that I learned from my Father I have made known to you" (John 15:14,15).

As Christians, we have a friendship in Jesus Christ. His friendship is far more comforting and helpful than any the Teacher could have known. The Teacher saw God as the ultimate judge, and so He is. But because Jesus has died to save us from condemnation, we see God as our loving Father, and so He is. Where the Teacher saw despair and hopelessness, we see victory. This new point of view is possible only because of the relationship we enjoy with God through Jesus Christ. It's incredible to think that for most of human history (those days before Jesus came), life was little more than "eat, drink and be merry, for tomorrow we die."

Before leaving this idea that Jesus is our friend, there is one last important point that must be made and understood. Remember that Jesus said, "You are my friends if you do what I command" (John 15:14). This indicates that we must work hard at developing our friendship with Him. His friendship is a gift, but we must labor to open the package and receive the full blessings of the gift. We must obey Him. I suspect that those Christians who aren't much interested in doing and being what Jesus commands will not have much interest in this chapter. But those believers who do love Jesus will rejoice in the contrast between the empty life of the wisest man on earth and the fullness that they themselves have received from the hand of their heavenly Friend.

The Teacher reminds us in Ecclesiastes 4:13-16 that fools forget their friends. He speaks of a person who started out wise enough to listen to those around him. But upon becoming a powerful king, he forgot the value of friendly advice and lost his friends. Both he and his successor were eventually rejected by their alienated friends and supporters.

Jesus the King will never forget those He calls His friends. Listen to how He prayed just before His arrest and crucifixion:

> *"Father, the time has come. Glorify your Son, that your Son may glorify you. For you granted him authority over all people that he might give eternal life to all those you have given him. Now this is eternal life: that they may know you, the only true God, and Jesus Christ, whom you have sent. I have brought you glory on earth by completing the work you gave me to do. And now, Father, glorify me in your presence with the glory I had with you before the world began."*
> John 17:1-5

Even as He faced death, Jesus remembered us. We will be in God's presence forever with Jesus Christ.

Some Lessons

There are several important lessons for living that can be gleaned from this section of Ecclesiastes. The foremost lesson is that life apart from God and Jesus is hardly worth mentioning. Only Jesus can lead us to the sort of living that God originally intended for us to enjoy.

Ecclesiastes also teaches us that we ought to take a stand against the injustices of this world. Perfect justice must wait for the end of history, but Christians should be at the forefront of all efforts to alleviate suffering and unfairness. We can't make the world a perfect place, but we can drag our feet as it spirals downward.

We can be friend and helper, offering comfort and support to those we meet. And we can be receptive to the support and guidance offered by others. Likewise, we should seek to cultivate our friendship with God by obedience to Jesus Christ. With God's comfort, support and guidance, we have the resources we need to deal with the injustices of this world.

Jesus is the proof that God will eventually prevail. Jesus was spat on, beaten, tortured, ridiculed, denied and crucified—but He came alive, conquering all the wrong heaped upon Him. When He returns in power and glory, it will be to heal the wounds of those who trust Him and to banish those who stand against Him.

1. Here's a "Great Doctrines of the Bible" quiz for you. Near the beginning of this chapter are quoted 1 Peter 1:3,4 and Romans 5:1,2,5. Find in those passages the following words and define them as you can: God, Father, Lord, Christ, mercy, new birth, hope, resurrection, dead, inheritance, heaven, justified, faith, peace with God, grace, glory, love, Holy Spirit. (You may want to check your definitions with a Bible dictionary.)

   Of what significance are each of these words to you?

2. "And now these three remain: faith, hope and love. But the greatest of these is love" (1 Cor. 13:13). In this chapter we talked about the hope that we have in God. Paul, in 1 Corinthians 13:13, names hope as one of three great things in the Christian's life. But Paul says the greatest is love. Someone once said that love is the greatest because, of the three, it alone will never change throughout eternity—love will always be love. What do you think faith and hope become when we finally arrive at heaven's gate?

3. Here's an interesting project for you to try. Watch the news on TV tonight and make a list of all the injustices you see. You can also look through the newspaper for headlines that list examples of man's inhumanity to man. Tomorrow list examples of justice and loving actions. Compare the two lists.

4. Name eight or ten examples of the sort of injustices you are likely to find in school. Do the same for injustices you are likely to find in the home. If you have a job, list some you might find there.

   Now think of practical ways you could deal with or help to eliminate some of these injustices.

5. Jesus said, "I tell you the truth, whatever you did for one of the least of these brothers of mine, you did for me" (Matt. 25:40).

What are some of the areas of service your youth group and church fellowship are involved in?

In what areas do you help?

In what areas could you help?

6. The Teacher compared people to animals and claimed that all go to dust. We said that for those people who have no faith and therefore no hope, this thought must seem distressingly accurate. What are some of the many ways that non-Christians try to avoid really believing that there is no life after death?

7. The Holy Spirit is God's comforter to us. Can you name some moments when the Spirit helped you? If not, what can you do to become more sensitive to God's Spirit?

Note

1. Eugene C. Roehlkepartain, ed., *The Youth Ministry Resource Book* (Loveland: Group Books, 1988), pp. 166,167.

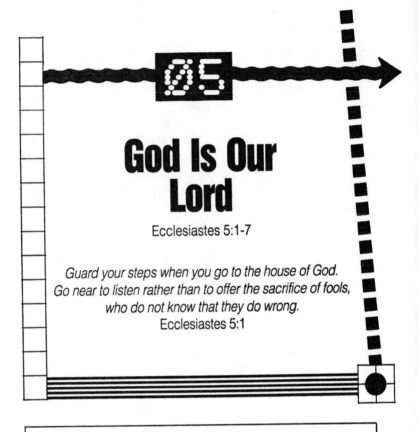

God Is Our Lord

Ecclesiastes 5:1-7

Guard your steps when you go to the house of God.
Go near to listen rather than to offer the sacrifice of fools,
who do not know that they do wrong.
Ecclesiastes 5:1

False worship is meaningless and is demonstrated by a lack of commitment to the Lord. Christians must strive to honor God with pure worship and steadfast commitment.

What's the worst thing that could happen to you? That's the question I asked my junior high Sunday School class. Perhaps you'd like to try the same survey that they filled out. Here it is:

There are twelve items in the list below. Place a *1* next to the item you would *least* like to have happen to you. Continue to number the items listed in the order you'd least like them to happen to you until

you've assigned each a number.
Having a bug fly up my nose.
Losing my legs.
Going blind.
Having a life-threatening addiction to drugs.
Having a family member die.
Becoming senile in old age.
Going to Sunday School.
Breaking up with someone I truly love.
Going off to war.
Not worshiping God with complete sincerity.
Having a friend who is severely burned.
Being poor.

Here are how the kids in my group rated the items:
1. Having a life-threatening addiction to drugs.
2. Not worshiping God with complete sincerity.
3. Going blind.
4. Having a family member die.
5. Losing my legs.
6. Having a friend who is severely burned.
7. Going off to war.
8. Becoming senile in old age.
9. Breaking up with someone I truly love.
10. Having a bug fly up my nose.
11. Being poor.
12. Going to Sunday School.

God would have slightly different answers, I suspect. Although He is certainly concerned for our physical well-being, it's the spiritual side of our existence that is most important to Him. To not worship God with sincerity is dangerous to your health. Why is that? Because true worship is commitment—giving your life to God is the highest form of worship. You can get to heaven if you're blind, without legs or even have a bug up your nose. But if your commitment to God is insincere you are in great spiritual peril. For without God there is no hope of finding meaning on earth or eternal life in heaven.

If you learn only one thing from the book of Ecclesiastes, it should be that God—not this world—is the true center of life and meaning. Your pleasure, pain, joys, sorrows, goals, high points and low points all take on more and more meaning as you draw closer to the Lord. The level of your commitment to God serves as an indicator of your success in finding meaning. Without God—without meaning.

One of Solomon's greatest motivations for writing Ecclesiastes was to show that indeed God is the center of life. Everything else is of little importance in comparison to Almighty God. In the passage we are going to look at now (Eccles. 5:1-7), Solomon, still in the guise of the Teacher, makes it plain that superficial worship is high on the list of meaningless things.

True Worship

Guard your steps when you go to the house of God. Go near to listen rather than to offer the sacrifice of fools, who do not know that they do wrong. Ecclesiastes 5:1

To fully understand the impact of the truth contained in this subtle verse, some terms must be defined.

Already mentioned is the idea that worshiping God is synonymous with giving your life to Him. Romans 12:1 says, "Therefore, I urge you, brothers, in view of God's mercy, to offer your bodies as living sacrifices, holy and pleasing to God—this is your spiritual act of worship." Paul, the author of Romans, felt that the act of giving oneself to God is a sacrifice—not in the sense of being a dead carcass prostrate on the altar, but as a human being alive to serve God with his or her every breath. Paul is pointing out that living in obedience to the Father is worship.

In Solomon's day, the people came to the Temple in Jerusalem to offer animal sacrifices as their act of worship. When the high priest went into the Most Holy Place in the inner Temple, God would appear to the priest as a visible light. The people began to think of the Temple as the place where God lived. When the Teacher said to "guard your steps when you go to the house of God," he was talking to people who literally traveled to visit God. Today, we know that there is no central place to find God. He is everywhere, and even lives within believers: "Don't you know that you yourselves are God's temple and that God's Spirit lives in you?" (1 Cor. 3:16). To us, "guard your steps" means to watch our behavior for God's sake. Since He is ever with us, we must always be certain to live as He would want us to.

The Teacher says to "go near to listen" to God. To listen to God means more than simply hearing. It means actively taking in what He is saying and obeying Him. Fools, the Teacher points out, don't listen to God and don't obey Him. In the Bible, a fool is not someone who is stupid but one who will not respond to the Lord.

The meaning of the verse, then, is this: *Watch your step. Make sure you lead a godly life and do what your Father tells you.* Many Christians try to skip this rule! Those Christians whose lives are centered on God rather than themselves are the ones who stand out from the crowd.

Mary and Martha

The story of Mary and Martha from Luke 10:38-42 illustrates the difference between a person who is centered on God and one who is not:

As Jesus and his disciples were on their way, he came to a village where a woman named Martha opened her home to him. She had a sister called Mary, who sat at the Lord's feet listening to what he said. But Martha was distracted by all the preparations that had to be made. She came to him and asked, "Lord, don't you care that my sister has left me to do the work by myself? Tell her to help me!"

"Martha, Martha," the Lord answered, "you are worried and upset about many things, but only one thing is needed. Mary has chosen what is better, and it will not be taken away from her."

Mary chose to sit and listen to Jesus. She listened, learned, felt His presence and enjoyed Him. Martha, on the other hand, had been running around trying to juggle all the details of the party. She wanted to entertain Jesus instead of listen to Him. If she had paid attention to Him, she would have learned that He just wanted to be near her and enjoy her company. The problem for Martha was that she, unlike Mary, was not centered on Jesus Christ. She was centered on the party. The party was too much for her to handle, so she became angry with Mary and upset with Jesus. Too many Christians have centered themselves on the party of life and all the things of the world, rather than simply placing themselves next to Jesus. This world is too much for anyone to handle. You can't juggle it and Jesus too as some Christians try to do.

The idea that God should be the center of our lives is forcefully brought home in a wonderful book by C.S. Lewis called *The Great Divorce*. It's a story about a bus trip that some people take from hell to heaven. They have come to see what heaven is like. They can even stay if they want to, but most don't because heaven hurts them. To the people from hell, everything in heaven is hard and heavy. Grass won't bend under their feet. Instead, it stabs them like ice picks. A leaf weighs as much as a load of bricks. Heaven is this way to them because heaven is true reality while hell is miserable meaninglessness. The people from hell are little more than transparent vapor with no weight or substance. To the citizens of heaven, though, the grass bends and the leaves are soft and beautiful.

There is a scene in *The Great Divorce* in which a woman named Pam, from hell, is talking to her brother Reginald, one of the citizens of heaven. Pam is complaining bitterly because she and her son Michael had been separated back on earth when Michael died at an early age. Pam claims that she is ready to leave hell and walk into heaven to see her son. There is a problem, however. Pam doesn't really care about heaven or God, she just wants her true love, Michael.

Reginald tells her, "But, Pam, do think! Don't you see you are not beginning at all as long as you are in that state of mind? You're treating God only as a means to Michael."

"If He loved me He'd let me see my boy," Pam replies. She goes on to say that she would be perfectly happy even in hell if she just had her son. "No one has a right to come between me and my son. Not even God. Tell Him that to His face. I want my boy, and I mean to have him. He is mine, do you understand? Mine, mine, mine, for ever and ever."

"He will be, Pam. Everything will be yours. God Himself will be yours. But not that way."[1]

To Pam, her love for Michael was noble and pure. But from a heavenly point of view it was pointless and corrupt because the center of her love was not God. If Pam had loved God her son would have been hers to enjoy forever.

Perhaps you enjoy speculating about heaven. What is it really like there? It's fun to imagine what it'll be like to live forever, to never have to sleep, to see all the angels, to talk with the disciples of Christ, to party and play and enjoy the sights. I must admit that I was guilty of looking forward to the experience of heaven perhaps more than I was looking forward to being with God. When I read the tale of Pam, I saw myself in her attitude. Now I'm trying to focus my desires on God alone. Everything else will be given as a gift—but it's the Giver, not the gift, that is important.

Meaningless Promises

Do not be quick with your mouth,
do not be hasty in your heart
to utter anything before God.
God is in heaven
and you are on earth,
so let your words be few.
As a dream comes when there are
many cares,
so the speech of a fool when there
are many words.
Ecclesiastes 5:2,3

In Solomon's time, when folks came to the Temple to offer sacrifices to the Lord, they would often make vows to Him. They would tell God something like, "Next time, it'll be TWO goats and our best ox," hoping to win His favor. The Teacher, however, was well aware that many of these promises were just hot air. That's why he cautions his readers, "When you make a vow to God, do not delay in fulfilling it. He has no pleasure in fools; fulfill your vow" (v. 4).

When Jesus died on the cross, His death paid the ultimate penalty for sin. As it says in the book of Hebrews, "He sacrificed for their sins once for all when he offered himself" (Heb. 7:27). Animal sacrifices are no longer necessary. (The Jews stopped the practice when Jerusalem was destroyed by the Romans shortly after Hebrews was written.)

God no longer requires animal sacrifices from His children, but it is clear that He does require sacrifices of an entirely different nature. See how well you match up in the sacrifice department by comparing yourself the following Bible passages.

Proverbs 21:3: "To do what is right and just is more acceptable to the Lord than sacrifice."

Hosea 6:6: "For I desire mercy, not sacrifice, and acknowledgment of God rather than burnt offerings."

Hebrews 13:16: "And do not forget to do good and to share with others, for with such sacrifices God is pleased."

1 Sam. 15:22: "Does the Lord delight in burnt offerings and sacrifices as much as in obeying the voice of the Lord? To obey is better than sacrifice, and to heed is better than the fat of rams."

These verses reveal that God wants us to do what is right and just, to show mercy, to center our lives on Him, to do good, to share with others and to obey God. It's obvious that the outward act of sacrifice is not important to our Lord. It is our inner selves—our character—that really matters. If we are filled with God's love, His love will flow out of us in tangible acts of justice, mercy and obedience. Obedience to God is really what the Teacher was demanding when he stated that vows made to the Lord must be kept.

The Ultimate Vow

Ecclesiastes 5:1-7 takes on real meaning for Christians when we apply it to our commitment to follow Jesus Christ. Our commitment is our vow to God—the most important vow that can be made.

Becoming a Christian is like being born. A true Christian is a happy, healthy little baby. But someone who makes an empty vow to follow Jesus is the same as a stillborn baby. An empty vow equals an empty commitment to God.

When a baby is born, he or she is given the parents' family name. In the same way, a person who vows to follow Jesus takes on God's family name. To be a stillborn Christian—one who doesn't really honor his or her vow to God—is to break the Third Commandment: "You shall not misuse the name of the Lord your God, for the Lord will not hold anyone guiltless who misuses his name" (Exod. 20:7). Stillborn Christians have ignored the Teacher's warnings by disregarding their vows to God.

Anyone who takes the name of the Lord as his or her own yet lives a life that dishonors Him is misusing His name.

There is a verse in Hebrews that ties together the two concepts of leading a life of sacrifices that please God and taking His name as one's own. Read Hebrews 13:15: "Through Jesus, therefore, let us continually offer to God a sacrifice of praise—the fruit of lips that confess his name." To confess God's name is to acknowledge Him as Lord and Savior; to make a vow of commitment to Him.

The Warning

Ecclesiastes 5:6 says, "Do not let your mouth lead you into sin." The Teacher was warning us to keep our commitment to God. A similar warning, directed at people who claimed to have committed their lives to God, is found in Hebrews 6:4-6:

It is impossible for those who have once been enlightened, who have tasted the heavenly gift, who have shared in the Holy Spirit, who have tasted the goodness of the word of God and the powers of the coming age, if they fall away, to be brought back to repentance, because to their loss they are crucifying the Son of God all over again and subjecting him to public disgrace.

The exact meaning of this passage has been debated by Christians. But it is certainly pointing out that the blessings God gives believers carry with them a responsibility. Christians must not "fall away from" the disciplines and teachings of their faith. The author of Hebrews goes on to say that God's promises are based on His own unchangeable nature. Therefore, those who put their hope in Jesus "have this hope as an anchor for the soul, firm and secure" (Heb. 6:19, see vv. 9-20 for more details).

Standards

Your commitment to Jesus Christ requires you to live by new standards. Just what are these standards? In this chapter alone we've mentioned quite a few things from the Bible: We should center ourselves on God; be living sacrifices; practice righteousness, justice, mercy, and obedience; and hold God's name in high honor. God's Word contains many more standards, but these are plenty for starters! How does your life measure up to these standards? Has your life changed since you became a Christian? Can your friends and family see any difference in you? Can you see any difference? Can *God* see any difference?

Imagine a large hunk of wax being melted in a pan. Once liquid, it can be poured into a mold to take the shape of the mold. The process of meeting the standards God has set is the process of being molded into the shape of Jesus Christ. Pity the poor Christian who wants to go back to his old pre-Christian shape—just a great hunk of wax with no real identity.

Jesus is our standard. It is our job and our privilege to become more and more like Him as we grow in our Christian faith. It's a life-long process and not an easy one. Happily, God does the work. Philippians 2:12,13 says, "Work out your salvation with fear and trembling, for it is God who works in you to will and to act according to his good purpose." To work out your salvation does not mean to work for it. It means to work because of it. Get growing! Become what God wants you to be. God will make the changes within you, but you must have the desire. Let Him mold you as He sees fit.

Standing in Awe of God

The Teacher closes this portion of his thoughts with, "Much dreaming and many words are meaningless. Therefore stand in awe of God" (Eccles. 5:7). God is awesome. Don't forget it.

Have too many of us forgotten it? Have we heard so many Bible studies, sat through so many services, spent so much time reading about Him that we've lost the thrill we feel in His presence? Have we become, like Lewis' character Pam, enthralled with the creation while forgetting the Creator? Are we the same as Martha, mixed up with the routine of this planet? Or do we share the nature of her sister Mary who just wanted to sit with Jesus? These questions bring us back to the main theme of Ecclesiastes 5:1-7: A superficial commitment to God, as reflected in unheeded vows, is meaningless. To get complete enjoyment from our own Christianity, we must center ourselves on God.

1. The survey at the beginning of the chapter listed "Not worshiping God with complete sincerity" as one of the terrible things in a list of terrible things. Now that you've read the chapter, define in detail what is meant by the phrase.

    Do you agree it is the worst thing on the list? Why or why not?

2. What is a fool? Imagine that you work for the "Construct-a-Fool" corporation. Your distasteful job is to assemble the parts that make up foolish people. You can find the parts in the following verses—look them up and list what you find: Psalm 14:1; Proverbs 1:7; 14:9; Romans 1:21; Galatians 6:3; Titus 3:3.

3. John 4:23 tells us, "Yet a time is coming and has now come when the true worshipers will worship the Father in spirit and truth, for they are the kind of worshipers the Father seeks." Now that you've read Ecclesiastes 5:1-7, how would you explain what Jesus meant by *true worshipers* and worshiping in *spirit* and in *truth*?

4. "If anyone considers himself religious and yet does not keep a tight rein on his tongue, he deceives himself and his religion is worthless" (Jas. 1:26). How does this compare with the Teacher's statement in Ecclesiastes 5:7?

   In addition to talking too much, a tongue can do many bad things. List five or six of them.

   Think up good things the tongue could do instead of the things on your list.

5. James 1:27 says, "Religion that God our Father accepts as pure and faultless is this: to look after orphans and widows in their distress and to keep oneself from being polluted by the world." This verse speaks of religion (or the worship of God) as a two part thing: service and personal purity. How does this relate to Ecclesiastes 5:1-7?

   What are some of the practical areas of service open to someone your age?

   What are some things of this world that threaten to pollute?

   How can you keep from being "polluted"?

6. It was said early in this chapter that if you learn only one thing from the book of Ecclesiastes, it should be that God—not the world—is the true center of a meaningful life. Imagine what sort of person you would be if God was truly the center of your life every moment, every day. How would you be different from what you are now?

   What is keeping you from being more like the person you imagined?

7. In what ways is committing your life to God similar to animal sacrifice?

   In what ways is it different? (See Romans 12:1 and other verses listed in this chapter for help.)

Note

1. C.S. Lewis, *The Great Divorce*, (New York: Macmillan, 1946), pp. 90, 92, 95.

God Is Our Treasure

Ecclesiastes 5:10-6:12

Then I realized that it is good and proper for a man to eat and drink, and to find satisfaction in his toilsome labor under the sun during the few days of life God has given him—for this is his lot.
Ecclesiastes 5:18

People who set out to get rich will probably never acquire enough wealth to satisfy them. In striving to become wealthy, they sacrifice contentment and their relationships with others.

When God created Adam and Eve, He endowed them with a long list of character traits that made up their perfect personalities. Though we have few details to tell us what His first people were like, we can assume they had love, curiosity, appreciation of God's creation and a thousand and one other parts and pieces.

When sin entered the picture, it destroyed Adam and Eve's special relationship with the Lord. Their innocence gone forever, they were banished from the garden. But the damage of sin didn't stop there. Sin took their God-given personality traits and bent them into spoiled versions of the originals.

We can see these bent traits in our own lives today. The perfect love with which Adam and Eve could love each other has become, due to sin, something closer to a clinging, self-centered thing. The trait that allowed Adam and Eve to innocently appreciate each other's beauty can be bent into lust. Healthy concern for the people and events around us degenerates into worries and fears. There are many other examples, for sin has affected each and every part of our being.

The book of Ecclesiastes provides a classic illustration of one good trait gone bad. God had given humanity a hunger for Him. But in many people that hunger has been corrupted into a competitive drive to acquire wealth and possessions. These people have lost the ability to identify their true need. They want the gifts instead of the Giver, much to their loss. In Ecclesiastes 5:10-6:12, the Teacher discusses this striving for wealth and the pain it brings to our world. As we study his thoughts, we'll find that the Teacher hit upon the one deadly change that sin has made in our hearts, the one corrupted trait from which all others stem: replacing God with self as the center of our affection.

Rich Fools

Whoever loves money never has money
enough;
whoever loves wealth is never
satisfied with his income.
This too is meaningless.
Ecclesiastes 5:10

Jesus had some very profound things to say about this subject. Let's take a look at Luke 12:13-21:

Someone in the crowd said to him, "Teacher, tell my brother to divide the inheritance with me."

Jesus replied, "Man, who appointed me a judge or an arbiter between you?" Then he said to them, "Watch out! Be on your guard against all kinds of greed; a man's life does not consist in the abundance of his possessions."

And he told them this parable: "The ground of a certain rich man produced a good crop. He thought to himself, 'What shall I do? I have no place to store my crops.'

"Then he said, 'This is what I'll do. I will tear down my barns and build bigger ones, and there I will store all my grain and my goods. And I'll say to myself, "You have plenty of good things laid up for many years. Take life easy; eat, drink and be merry."'

"But God said to him, 'You fool! This very night your life will be demanded from you. Then who will get what you have prepared for yourself?'

"This is how it will be with anyone who stores up things for himself but is not rich toward God."

The rich fool was preoccupied with wealth. In essence, he was trying to be his own god. He was enthroned at the center of his life. This is a common condition for unsaved people. They may achieve wealth, but they are poverty stricken in the area of their relationship with God. Jesus made it plain that life is more than money. "A man's life does not consist in the abundance of his possessions," He said in verse 15. From God's point of view, life is eternal. The things we seek to own have nothing at all to do with eternal life since they are temporary and are soon left behind.

For those of us who are saved, materialism still presents a very real threat. Jesus said, "You cannot serve both God and Money" (Matt. 6:24). A Christian must focus his or her desires on God, not possessions. The results of becoming more interested in money than in God are detailed in 1 Timothy 6:10:

For the love of money is a root of all kinds of evil. Some people, eager for money, have wandered from the faith and pierced themselves with many griefs.

But I'm Not Rich

You may not feel that you have a problem with money. But the same attitude that is at the root of materialism can show up in other ways. It is an attitude of valuing anything more than God. Anything that comes between you and God—whether it's a desire for cash, popularity, good looks, power, influence or any other thing—is a form of idolatry. Even if you don't care a bit about money, Ecclesiastes and the other Scriptures apply to you.

A couple of weeks ago I asked my junior high Sunday School students to list the things that people their age generally consider to be marks of success. They listed wealth, fame, good looks and achieving goals. The same sort of stuff people of all ages would list.

"Good," I told them, pleased at their reply. But then I was surprised at their response to my next question.

I said, "Wouldn't you agree that all these things could be summed up in one word: Happiness? Isn't happiness the true goal that we all seek, and these things you've listed are just means to that goal?"

Their response surprised me—they had no response at all. They stared back at me with blank expressions, as if they hadn't heard what I'd said.

So I attempted to explain myself. "See, happiness is what people really want in life. Wealth, good looks and all the rest are the things people hope will bring happiness. Wouldn't you agree?"

Normally, the kids in my class are very alert and quick to join in. Yet still they eyeballed me in motionless silence, looking at me glassily and saying nothing. It was a bit disconcerting. I remembered a Twilight Zone episode in which a man had an odd problem with words. He was surrounded by people who used the wrong words. When his wife asked him if he wanted lunch, he heard her say, "Do you want me to fix you some encyclopedia?" I thought I had said "happiness," but maybe it came out "broken legs" or something. Unfortuantely, that was not the case. The kids simply did not comprehend what I was talking about.

The incident seemed odd to me. It was as if the students had never thought about actually trying to attain happiness. The idea of being happy appeared so new and foreign to their thinking that they could not even respond to the suggestion of happiness. To them, wealth, good looks, popularity and the rest are not means to the goal of happiness, they *are* the goals.

Has our society become so spiritually bankrupt that we don't even look to riches to bring us happiness—we just want to possess the riches? If so, we have a very far distance to travel to find the real source of happiness: Jesus Christ.

How to Get Rich

Our man Solomon, speaking as the Teacher, describes some of the ins and outs of worldly wealth in Ecclesiastes 5:10-17. You can read the passage from your Bible. Briefly, it says that as a person earns more bucks, frivolous expenses also increase to consume them (v. 11), wealth brings anxiety and sleepless nights (v. 12), hoarded wealth can be harmful (v. 13), it can be lost (v. 14) and none of it can be taken into eternity (vv. 15-17).

Not all of these frustrations are automatic results of wealth. Not every rich person is miserable. The Teacher is just trying to point out that money is far from a guarantee of happiness.

Once again Jesus had some very wise advice on the matter:

"Do not store up for yourselves treasures on earth, where moth and rust destroy, and where thieves break in and steal. But store up for yourselves treasures in heaven, where moth and rust do not destroy, and where thieves do not break in and steal. For where your treasure is, there your heart will be also.

"The eye is the lamp of the body. If your eyes are good, your whole body will be full of light. But if your eyes are bad, your whole body will be full of darkness. If then the light within you is darkness, how great is that darkness!

"No one can serve two masters. Either he will hate the one and love the other, or he will be devoted to the one and despise the other. You cannot serve both God and Money"
Matthew 6:19-24

Christ's advice can be summarized in three main points: (1) Seek heavenly wealth. (2) Longing for earthly wealth will darken your understanding, like wearing dark glasses will reduce your vision. (Riches can deaden your sensitivity to God.) (3) It's impossible to split your devotions. God will not share the throne with your bank account.

This raises a few questions, two of which we will examine here: What is heavenly treasure? How do we earn it?

It is impossible to completely answer the first question. What are the treasures we receive in heaven? The Bible doesn't give a lot of details, but when it does talk about heaven it usually describes it in terms of earthly riches! That is, it speaks of streets of gold, foundations of precious stones and gates of giant pearls (see Rev. 21). If these are literal descriptions of heaven, then we will share wealth beyond our wildest imagination. If they are earthly symbols to describe spiritual things too grand for our ability to conceive, than we will be a million times richer than our wildest imagination! Either way, it sure beats any wealth we might have now.

But there are other treasures in heaven—we can capture a faint image of them here on earth. Love will be there. Love beyond anything we could ever experience here. Victory will be there, the victory over all the old sins and foolishness of this life. Health will be there. The pains and handicaps, the ravages of age that are so apparent in this life, will all be things of the past. And, yes, happiness will be there. The happiness we all seek will be there to welcome us with open arms and a hearty, never-ending embrace. For God is the source of all these things, and He is there to embrace us.

Before we go on to the second question, let's take a look at the different natures of the two types of riches: earthly and heavenly. As both Teachers—Jesus and Solomon—pointed out, earthly riches are fleeting. Heavenly wealth hangs in there.

Money spent is money gone; love spent is love gained. That's the difference between the two types of wealth. Heavenly riches reproduce themselves and bring great joy. Earthly riches fail. This is one reason why heaven provides the meaning in life that this planet does not.

After he discussed the problems faced by people who want to get rich (see 1 Tim. 6:9,10), the apostle Paul listed some of the spiritual riches that Christ may have had in mind when He told us to store up treasures in heaven.

Paul said, "Pursue righteousness, godliness, faith, love, endurance and gentleness" (v. 11). All these things describe the sort of personality traits we will enjoy in heaven. We earn them by practicing them here on earth. On earth these things are verbs; we do them. In heaven they are nouns; we receive them. Today we act good. Tomorrow we are good.

Paul continued:

Command those who are rich in this present world not to be arrogant or to put their hope in wealth, which is so uncertain, but to put their hope in God, who richly provides us with everything for our enjoyment. Command them to do good, to be rich in good deeds, and to be generous and willing to share. In this way they will lay up treasure for themselves as a firm foundation for the coming age, so that they may take hold of the life that is truly life. 1 Timothy 6:17-19

This answers our second question, "How do we earn heavenly treasure?" is *hope in God* (center your life on God) and *do good things*.

The Coin in the Treasure Box

Let's move on to the next passage in Ecclesiastes:

Then I realized that it is good and proper for a man to eat and drink, and to find satisfaction in his toilsome labor under the sun during the few days of life God has given him—for this is his lot. Moreover, when God gives any man wealth and possessions, and enables him to enjoy them, to accept his lot and be happy in his work—this is a gift of God. He seldom reflects on the days of his life, because God keeps him occupied with gladness of heart. Ecclesiastes 5:18-20

Here is the Teacher's prescription for satisfaction. The Teacher reveals the key to his treasure chest.

Forget the pursuit of wealth, he says. God will make you rich if He wants to. In the meantime, enjoy what you have, enjoy your work and enjoy life, for these are all gifts from God. And, he adds, be occupied with God.

The true wisdom and attitude of Solomon seem to be breaking through here. Notice the difference between the "Meaningless! Meaningless!" (Eccles. 1:2) worldly "under the sun" attitude compared with Solomon's attitude of gratefulness for and enjoyment of God's precious gifts. This contrast, then, is Solomon's way of getting his message through. After explaining that happiness cannot be found in materialism, he shows that happiness is found in God.

The Rejected Gift

In several statements about finding pleasure in life, the Teacher identifies God as the source of satisfaction and enjoyment:

A man can do nothing better than to eat and drink and find satisfaction in his work. This too, I see, is from the hand of God, for without him, who can eat or find enjoyment? Ecclesiastes 2:24,25

I know that there is nothing better for men than to be happy and do good while they live. That everyone may eat and drink, and find satisfaction in all his toil—this is the gift of God. Ecclesiastes 3:12,13

Then I realized that it is good and proper for a man to eat and drink, and to find satisfaction in his toilsome labor under the sun during the few days of life God has given him—for this is his lot. Ecclesiastes 5:18

But the Teacher throws a monkey wrench in the works:

I have seen another evil under the sun, and it weighs heavily on men: God gives a man wealth, possessions and honor, so that he lacks nothing his heart desires, but God does not enable him to enjoy them, and a stranger enjoys them instead. Ecclesiastes 6:1,2

What he is saying is this, "Yes, God gives terrific gifts—but that doesn't mean we will necessarily enjoy them." There are a million reasons why a person might not enjoy life. Ill health, war, a rotten little brother—whatever the case, people will forever find reasons large and small to miss the full pleasure that life can afford. Sad but true.

Our emotions are controlled so much by our circumstances. I've seen healthy, well-off people collapse in fits of sobs and anger because their football team blew an "important" game. Six months after one baseball team lost the play-offs, I heard two guys in an elevator bitterly bewailing their team's defeat. They weren't joking. These guys, half a year later, were still distraught and depressed. Maybe they lost money on the deal, I don't know. But it was my team that beat theirs. I didn't tell them that because I really and truly thought they would punch me, they were so upset.

Circumstances cannot always be controlled or avoided. However, a person who is centered on the Lord can smile through the tears and trials, knowing that there is a purpose and, eventually, an end.

In Ecclesiastes 6:3-6, the Teacher moves on to true tragedies that sometimes must be faced:

A man may have a hundred children and live many years; yet no matter how long he lives, if he cannot enjoy his prosperity and does not receive proper burial, I say that a stillborn child is better off then he. It comes without meaning, it departs in darkness, and in darkness its name is shrouded. Though it never saw the sun or knew anything, it has more rest than does that man—even if he lives a thousand years twice over but fails to enjoy his prosperity. Do not all go to the same place?

In those days, having a hundred kids would be considered a good thing! It was a mark of economic security and status in the community. Long years would also be considered a blessing. But if the person can't enjoy his life even though he has many blessings and if he dies dishonored and unlamented, then he is in worse shape than a baby born dead. To a person without God, life is a meaningless trip to extinction and oblivion.

Ecclesiastes 6:7-9 lists additional things to worry about.

The reason the average person worries about the events of life is that they seek security in the wrong things. People seek security in parents, jobs, spouses, bank accounts, political leaders and who knows what else. But they are like bowling pins holding hands while the ball is coming, because all earthly things are too weak to offer complete protection. Things that seem secure will eventually fail.

Jesus described a fool who built his house on the sand. It probably looked great, but it fell with a thud when the storms came. The wise man built on the rock of God's promises, and his house withstood difficult times (see Matt. 7:24-29). A life built on the sand of this world will slide into the abyss, but the life based on God will achieve victory.

Jesus also talked about the futility of worry:

> *"Therefore I tell you, do not worry about your life, what you will eat or drink; or about your body, what you will wear. Is not life more important than food, and the body more important than clothes? Look at the birds of the air; they do not sow or reap or stow away in barns, and yet your heavenly Father feeds them. Are you not much more valuable than they? Who of you by worrying can add a single hour to his life?"*
> Matthew 6:25-27

Nobody, by worrying, can add a single hour to his or her life. But eternal life can be added through Jesus Christ.

People choose to worry, however. The Teacher was doing it three thousand years ago, the people listening to Jesus were doing it two thousand years ago, and we're still at it today. But the truth is, there is no real reason to worry. God is in control. And even if He wasn't, worry wouldn't change anything anyway!

What do people your age fret about? Maybe it's appearance, friends, family problems, school or any other of a long list of things real and imaginary. Just remember, if you worry about these things, it's because you choose to be worried about them. You cannot change anything with nervous perspiration. God has given you the freedom to put your faith in His control. Take advantage of that gift.

Worry Versus Concern

Some of you are probably thinking, *Come on, we have to be concerned about the troubles we face*. True. But healthy concern is something completely different than worry:

> Concern tends to be directed outward—
> you care about others.
> Worry is self-centered—you fret about yourself.
> Concern takes action—you try to put things right.
> Worry paralyzes—you tend to give up.
> Concern is generous—you give of yourself.
> Worry is miserly—you cling to your personal
> security blanket.
> Concern looks to God for the solution.
> Worry doubts God.
> Concern is a strength.
> Worry is a weakness.
> Concern is a comfort to others.
> Worry is a hassle to others.
> Concern is good for you.
> Worry can stress you out.
> Concern is a God-given trait.
> Worry is a trait bent by sin.

Pretty amazing what a little sinfulness can do to a trait, eh? Multiply that by the hundreds of traits and emotions that make up a personality and it's plain to see why we need a Savior to rescue and heal us!

God Is in Control

The Teacher recognized that God is in ultimate control. He said, "Whatever exists has already been named, and what man is has been known; no man can contend with one who is stronger than he" (Eccles. 6:10). To put it another way, God has predetermined our circumstances, foreknew us and our attitudes and is strong enough to carry out His will. Knowing that, and knowing that God loves us, gives us confidence to face life with a bit of a smile.

For who knows what is good for a man in life, during the few and meaningless days he passes through like a shadow? Who can tell him what will happen under the sun after he is gone? Ecclesiastes 6:12

God knows what's good for us. He knows what will happen on earth after we leave it. And He has revealed some of that knowledge to us: Jesus is good for us, and Jesus is coming back in power and glory someday, bringing the riches of heaven to all believers still on earth.

A Final Thought

We worry about a lot of things in life. The Teacher was concerned about the many problems we face in trying to build our security upon this world's riches. But all the calamities that can befall our worldly possessions and goals can't do the slightest damage to heavenly riches. Look at Galatians 5:22,23:

But the fruit of the Spirit is love, joy, peace, patience, kindness, goodness, faithfulness, gentleness and self-control. Against such things there is no law.

These are enormously valuable gifts from God. But the greatest treasure God has given us is His love. And we can rely on that love:

For I am convinced that neither death nor life, neither angels nor demons, neither the present nor the future, nor any

powers, neither height nor depth, nor anything else in all crea-
tion, will be able to separate us from the love of God that is in
Christ Jesus our Lord.
Romans 8:38,39

These are very special promises from God's Word. They provide direct and powerful solutions to the problems that accompany materialism pointed out by the Teacher. They are guides to true riches. I hope you make them your own.

1. Here are some personality traits that God created for us to enjoy: Love, loyalty, trust, inner peace, humor and honesty. How might sin corrupt and "bend" these traits into negative characteristics? (Example: love can be bent into lust.)
   Jesus is the perfect model for all these traits as God intended them to be. How can you be more like Jesus?

2. Compare your thoughts and motivations to those listed in the "Worry Versus Concern" section of this chapter. Are you a concerned citizen or a worrier?

3. Read 1 Timothy 6:6-10. Match each verse with verses that express similar ideas in Ecclesiastes 5:10-6:12.

4. A survey reported that teenage girls spend 24.3 percent of their income on clothes, 23.1 percent on personal grooming, 7.8 percent on movies, dating and entertainment, 8.0 percent for car and gasoline, 7.1 percent for food and snacks, and the rest on various junk. (Guys' percentages for the same things are 15.2, 6.4, 16.6, 15.9 and 12.3 respectively.)[1] Try to add up your budget and see how it compares.
   What does this teach you about the things you consider to be "treasures" here on earth?

5. Do you contribute to a church or charity?

If you do, what percentage of your income do you tend to give?

If you don't, at what point would you be willing to give regularly?

6. "You cannot serve both God and Money" (Matt. 6:24) can be rephrased to say "You can't live for this world and live for the next." What are some of the spiritual dangers of sitting on the fence between this world and what God wants?

What are some of the attractions of this world that seem to draw Christians away from God?

What would you say to a friend who seems to be more concerned with his or her income and possessions than with God?

7. List at least five practical things that you could do this week to "store up riches in heaven" (see Matt. 6:20). (When we say practical, we mean something that you would actually want to do for friends or family, not something like, "Hand out Bibles at the Sports Arena"!)

Note
1. Eugene C. Rochlkepartain, ed., *The Youth Ministry Resource Book* (Loveland: Group Books, 1988), p. 88.

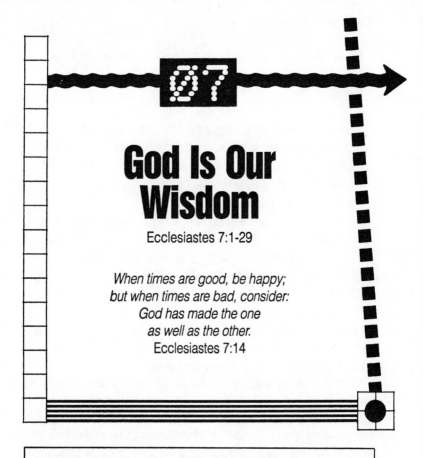

God Is Our Wisdom

Ecclesiastes 7:1-29

When times are good, be happy;
but when times are bad, consider:
God has made the one
as well as the other.
Ecclesiastes 7:14

In this life all people will face difficulties. In times of trouble, wisdom and faith produce spiritual growth in believers.

By this time, you are probably thinking, *Wow! This book of Ecclesiastes is a real downer!* Let's face it—the Teacher is not the kind of fun-loving happy-go-lucky, yuk-a-minute guy you'd want to entertain at your next birthday party.

Why is Ecclesiastes so negative? Maybe we can answer our questions by thinking for a minute about what was going on in Solomon's life. Let's look at a few revealing passages:

Men of all nations came to listen to Solomon's wisdom, sent by all the kings of the world, who had heard of his wisdom.
1 Kings 4:34

When the queen of Sheba heard of Solomon's fame, she came to Jerusalem to test him with hard questions . . . . Solomon answered all her questions; nothing was too hard for him to explain to her. 2 Chronicles 9:1,2

All the kings of the earth sought audience with Solomon to hear the wisdom God had put in his heart. Year after year, everyone who came brought a gift—articles of silver and gold, and robes, weapons and spices, and horses and mules. 2 Chronicles 9:23,24

Year after year Solomon was being plied with questions. Incessant questions. Questions without let up, never ending, devoid of coffee breaks, lined up twice around the block.

And it's safe to assume the questions were all the same. Day after day, the same old unoriginal questions were probably asked: "Solomon! What new thing will happen tomorrow?" "Oh, King—live forever—how can I achieve wisdom or pleasure or accomplishments?" "Tell me how I can know if I should make war or peace with my neighboring kingdoms?" "How can I get the god of my country on my side?" "How can I become richer?"

How would you feel after a few decades of that? Solomon may have thrown up his hands and said, "Listen, you turkeys! You're each asking me to tell you how you can take control of your life. You can't do it! What do you want from me? God is the one in control. You ask me what will happen tomorrow. Don't worry about it. As far as I know nothing new will happen tomorrow—there is nothing new under the sun. You want wisdom, pleasure and achievement? Good luck—without God it's all meaningless, a chasing after the wind. War or peace? How should I know—God has made a time and season for everything. You want God on your side? Keep your vows and worship Him. You want to get richer? Fine—the pursuit of it will wreck your life."

Solomon recognized that there was one basic and fundamental answer to all the questions: The people needed to trust God and let Him handle the show.

No one can realistically hope to have control over anything that goes on in life. Only God can do that. "Just put God at the center of your life and enjoy whatever He gives you" is the primary truth of what Solomon knew to be the ultimate wisdom.

But now we can imagine another problem Solomon had to deal with: "Just put God at the center of your life" doesn't satisfy most people. They say, "Oh, right. Sure, Solomon—but c'mon, what is the *real* secret?" Apparently, the people of Solomon's day didn't want to settle for what they felt God had to offer. Even today, there are few who put their trust in the Lord.

So perhaps he began to write the book of Ecclesiastes to help answer their questions. And it's negative because it's telling people that their struggles to obtain all the things they want in life are useless. Self-centered struggles were something the experienced Solomon knew to be completely futile and meaningless in light of what God offers.

Wisdom in Seven Easy (?) Lessons

Now we come to the seventh chapter of Ecclesiastes. Solomon has answered all the questions put to him. He's even injected a little description of the good life on earth:

> *Moreover, when God gives any man wealth and possessions, and enables him to enjoy them, to accept his lot and be happy in his work—this is a gift of God. He seldom reflects on the days of his life, because God keeps him occupied with gladness of heart.*
> Ecclesiastes 5:19,20

Solomon knew that happiness is found in God. Be occupied with God, he counseled. Be God-centered. That's the wise thing.

Having established that without God, all is meaningless, Solomon moved on to describe how people can build on the foundation of a life centered on God. He gave seven principles of godly wisdom.

ONE: A wise person must cultivate a good reputation.

A good name is better than fine
perfume,
and the day of death better than the
day of birth.
It is better to go to a house of mourning
than to go to a house of feasting,
for death is the destiny of every
man;
the living should take this to heart.
Ecclesiastes 7:1,2

The Teacher asks us to compare and contrast a good name to fine perfume. They are alike in that they both are pleasant, valuable and draw favorable attention to their owner. They are different in that one can be easily purchased at a store but the other must be earned. Also, perfume wears off shortly while a good name is enhanced over time.

The Teacher linked a good name with death and mourning because those things are what really bring out the true nature of a name.

It's fairly easy to be a popular person when times are happy. When the economy is healthy, it's common for employees to respect their employers. But when the situation changes and management starts cutting wages and laying off people while still driving their limousines to their exclusive country clubs—that makes for a bad name in a big hurry. To earn and keep a good name requires kindness, fairness and generosity even during troubled times. Solomon's audience of worldly kings and queens may have had to check the royal dictionaries for the meanings of kindness, fairness and generosity.

TWO: Hard times teach us more than happy times.

Have you ever been to a funeral service? I attended the grave-side service of a boy in my youth group who died of leukemia. Hundreds of people came and the tears flowed like rain. Sermons were made, prayers were whispered, new leaves were turned. We all left that day thinking about the meaning of life and our own mortality.

I'm sure the boy's day of birth had much less impact than his day of death. Nobody came to see him arrive except his mom, a doctor or nurse and a few members of his immediate family. It was a joyful time, but much less instructive than the suffering caused by his departure.

A person grows wise when he or she confronts difficult times. The boy's family was brought to a new awareness of God, life and the futility of trying to control and change things. The boy's friends also had the light begin to dawn on them. And the boy himself grew greatly nearer to the Lord as his time on earth decreased.

He had been a nice kid to have in the youth group, but not greatly involved and certainly not one I would have characterized as "on fire for Jesus." Yet shortly before his death, he called several of his friends and told them one by one that the sort of life-style (partying, drinking and so forth) he and they had shared was destructive. He let them know that they needed to give themselves completely to the Lord Jesus Christ. That's wisdom. It took a whole lot of suffering to gain it.

THREE: A wise person is refined by sorrow.

Sorrow is better than laughter,
because a sad face is good for the
heart.
The heart of the wise is in the house of
mourning,
but the heart of fools is in the house
of pleasure.
Ecclesiastes 7:3,4

Although Solomon's intention was to show how tough it is to

acquire the wisdom that propels us to God (who is the foundation of all true wisdom), his words clearly apply to those of us who already cling to the Lord. The New Testament writers had more to say on the subject of sorrow and suffering:

> *No discipline seems pleasant at the time, but painful. Later on, however, it produces a harvest of righteousness and peace for those who have been trained by it.*
> Hebrews 12:11

> *Consider it pure joy, my brothers, whenever you face trials of many kinds, because you know that the testing of your faith develops perseverance. Perseverance must finish its work so that you may be mature and complete, not lacking anything.*
> James 1:2-4

In a person who is sustained by God, sorrow can produce righteousness, peace, perseverance, maturity, completeness and fullness, plus the good heart mentioned in the Ecclesiastes passage. These traits characterize a truly wise person.

FOUR: Criticism and wise advice are better than praise.

> *It is better to heed a wise man's*
> > *rebuke*
> *than to listen to the song of fools.*
> *Like the crackling of thorns under the*
> > *pot,*
> *so is the laughter of fools.*
> *This too is meaningless.*
> > Ecclesiastes 7:5,6

In Jesus' time, the religious life was presided over primarily by two fraternities of select men known as the Pharisees and Sadducees. Together, they controlled every aspect of the faith, including all the rituals, special celebrations, teaching duties and Temple operations. Because of their important position in the religious life of the society, they were highly regarded by the community. They were the guys with the power.

Jesus characterized them (particularly the Pharisees, who thought themselves to be the more pious and godly) as pompous, prideful, blind, wicked, empty, hypocritical and condemned to hell. (See Matthew 23 for the Lord's incredibly hard biting harangue against the teachers of the law and the Pharisees.)

These men, professing to be wise, were fools. They loved to hear praise. They hated to hear criticism, even when it came from the mouth of the very Messiah they longed to see but failed to recognize. Thoroughly insulted by Jesus and unable to appreciate the wisdom in His critique, they planned and brought about His crucifixion within the week.

No one likes criticism. But to consider it when it does come and to make positive changes in response to it is a requirement for becoming wise.

FIVE: The wise don't allow dishonesty into their lives.
> *Extortion turns a wise man into a fool,*
> *and a bribe corrupts the heart.*
>> Ecclesiastes 7:7

Many Bible scholars have claimed that this verse is a mistake— that some scribe somewhere along the line got mixed up and accidentally wrote this in where it doesn't belong. They say this because they don't understand that Solomon is speaking to kings and queens who have come to him thinking they want to find the way to wisdom. Sadly this verse was very appropriate for many kings and queens of Solomon's day, for many of them were the personifications of corruption! Bribes and extortions were their daily routine. They had bribes for breakfast, ill-gotten loot for lunch, payola for dinner and hush money to sleep on.

This step to wisdom must have been a hard one for the rotten rulers to swallow. By this time, some may have been saying, "Now wait just a second! You mean I have to suffer, be miserable, open myself to criticism and be *honest* on top of it all?"

Exactly. The wise person avoids sin. The wise man and woman don't live like the rest of the world does. They don't allow dishonesty to wreck their lives, the Teacher says. This supports the idea that God must be at the center of our affections, not money or any other thing.

SIX: The wise avoid worry and anger and channel their energy into working for a solution.

The end of the matter is better than its
beginning,
and patience is better than pride.
Do not be quickly provoked in your
spirit,
for anger resides in the lap of fools.
Ecclesiastes 7:8,9

Solomon admonishes his imperial clientele to put down their stubborn pride and arrogance and accept things with patience. Patience is one of the character traits God intended for us to have. It is a gift of the Spirit (see Gal. 5:22) and it is an element of love (see 1 Cor. 13:4).

Patience is often translated as "long-suffering." We see the idea of suffering—putting up with or dealing with—in this word.

Solomon is saying that the wise person, instead of fretting and worrying about the way things are or exploding in anger, will channel his or her intense emotional drives into action. The wise person responds to his or her problems by helping and working toward a solution.

SEVEN: Take charge of today.

Do not say, "Why were the old days
better than these?"
For it is not wise to ask such
questions.
Ecclesiastes 7:10

This verse mentions one of those great questions muttered in the cold chill of discouragement and frustration: "Why can't today be better?" This question is sometimes rephrased as "Why is this happening to me?" or "Why is God allowing this to happen?" or just plain "WHY?"

The Teacher has covered a lot of paper trying to give the answer, which is basically, "Uh, well . . . I really don't know. But God knows, so trust Him." At first, this answer may appear to be a copout, but in fact it is the only answer we need. Trust God. Isn't knowing that God will work things out better than only knowing why things happen? Actually, *God* is why things happen. He may let us know the reasons when He's ready.

It seems, however, that people have always had difficulty trusting God. When things are going badly they long for the "good old days." Nine times out of ten, the old days weren't any better anyway. Memories of the past are often faulty. To dwell on the past is foolishness. As the Teacher would say, it is a "chasing after wind." The past has blown behind us. Therefore, Solomon's point is "Take charge of today." Nothing can be done about yesterday. But within the range of control that God does allow us in our lives, we can take responsibility for today. This is real wisdom. Don't sit on your overstuffed throne and say, "Well, there goes the old ball game." Get up and do something. A wise person is an involved person.

The High Schooler's Response

To sum up, here are the seven principles of wisdom described by the Teacher: Earn and keep a good name, learn from suffering, learn from sorrow, heed criticism, be honest, channel worry and anger into positive action and take charge of today.

What do these things mean to a Christian your age? If you are in high school like most readers of this book, you'll want to know how you can milk the good stuff that applies to your age group out of Solomon's thoughts. How can all this advice be applied to your situation? Why don't we brainstorm a list of practical things you can do to gain wisdom? These are just a few ideas to get your thinking started.

Earn a good name:

Be kind to the unpopular kids.

Watch your tongue—don't gossip, lie, swear or unduly criticize.

Invite kids to youth group or other fun events.

Reject the "Party Animal" philosophy.

Learn from suffering and sorrow:

Draw near to God for comfort.

Seek the advice of mature Christians.

Study what the Bible says about sorrow and pain.

Ask yourself if your suffering is caused by something you shouldn't be doing. Stop doing it.

Heed criticism and wise advice:

Always compare advice to the truth found in the Bible.

If you disagree with a criticism, ask a mature Christian for a second opinion.

Don't just wait for advice, seek it out from people and reliable books.

Don't procrastinate about any changes you need to make.

Live honestly:

Don't let peer pressure push you into doing things you know are wrong.

Stand up for what you believe.

Be truthful.

Be sexually above reproach.

Work for solutions:

Get involved in youth group service projects.

Help plan new projects.

Set up a plan to faithfully contribute a portion of your income to the youth group or charity, even if you have little to share.

When you are angry or worried, seek the advice of a mature Christian.

Take charge of today:

Be an active participant, not just an observer.

Center your life on God.

Don't dwell on the way things might have been, dwell on the things of God.

If you've made mistakes, ask for and accept God's forgiveness; determine not to make the same mistake again; then get on with life.

One Advantage

Wisdom, like an inheritance, is a good
*   thing*
*   and benefits those who see the sun.*
Wisdom is a shelter
*   as money is a shelter,*
but the advantage of knowledge is this:
*   that wisdom preserves the life of its*
*   possessor.*
*   Consider what God has done:*
Who can straighten
*   what he has made crooked?*
When times are good, be happy;
*   but when times are bad, consider:*
*   God has made the one*
*   as well as the other.*
*   Therefore, a man cannot discover*
*   anything about his future.*
*   Ecclesiastes 7:11-14*

Notice how this passage compares to the passage in Ecclesiastes 1:13-15:

I devoted myself to study and to explore by wisdom all that is done under heaven. What a heavy burden God has laid on men! I have seen all the things that are done under the sun; all of them are meaningless, a chasing after the wind.

> *What is twisted cannot be*
> *straightened;*
> *what is lacking cannot be counted.*

The two passages are similar in that they discuss wisdom and the impossibility of trying to straighten out what God has made crooked. But look at the different attitudes toward wisdom. In 1:13,14, the Teacher calls wisdom meaningless. In 7:11,12, he calls it a good thing, able to preserve life!

Why did he seem to change his tune so drastically? The best answer may be that by chapter seven Solomon felt he had adequately defined true wisdom as opposed to the shallow, human, "under the sun" wisdom his followers were interested in. Their wisdom was self-centered and based on earthly understanding. Solomon's wisdom was God-centered and based on heavenly truth. It's this superior wisdom to which the Teacher is referring when he describes its advantage: protection that really works.

The Teacher goes on to imply that God knows what is best and we can't change certain things. The greatest wisdom cannot change what God has set. So stop struggling and enjoy life.

The Righteous

> *In this meaningless life of mine I*
> *have seen both of these:*
> *a righteous man perishing in his*
> *righteousness,*
> *and a wicked man living long in his*
> *wickedness.*
> *Do not be overrighteous,*
> *neither be overwise—*
> *why destroy yourself?*
> *Do not be overwicked,*
> *and do not be a fool—*
> *why die before your time?*
> *It is good to grasp the one*
> *and not let go of the other.*

The man who fears God will avoid
all extremes.
Ecclesiastes 7:15-18

Don't be overwise or overrighteous? Now what sort of monkey wrench is the Teacher throwing in the works? The whole idea of Ecclesiastes is to bring people to true wisdom!

To understand this portion of Scripture, let's start from the bottom and go up. The Teacher says that "The man who fears God will avoid all extremes." That can be paraphrased as "The person centered on God will stay close to Him."

The Teacher says to not be overrighteous, overwise or overwicked. This could be paraphrased as "Don't be legalistic and don't be loose."

And the Teacher says he has seen a righteous man perish and a wicked man prosper. He uses this observation to prove his point, which is that a person should depend on God, not on his own personal legalistic righteousness. He should depend on God, not his own human wisdom. He should depend on God, rather than reject Him for a life of wickedness.

Wisdom makes one wise man more
powerful
than ten rulers in a city.
There is not a righteous man on earth
who does what is right and never
sins.
Ecclesiastes 7:19,20

One wise man attached to Jesus is more powerful than any kingly army from earth or hell. Even righteousness cannot save, the Teacher implies, because really no one is righteous. A wise man is attached to God and is victorious where all of earth's righteous people combined fall in defeat.

Jesus showed the truth of this when He challenged a rich ruler to give up his wealth and position to follow Him. Because the ruler was so materially blessed, all the onlookers figured that he must be a real man of God. But when he declined the Lord's offer, Jesus said, "I tell you the truth, it is hard for a rich man to enter the kingdom of heaven. Again I tell you, it is easier for a camel to go through the eye of a needle than for a rich man to enter the kingdom of God" (Matt. 19:23,24).

This declaration blew the sandals off the disciples. They were astonished, the Bible says, and wanted to know who then could be saved (see Matt. 19:25). In their minds, people became wealthy and powerful because God rewarded their righteousness. If those blessed by God couldn't be saved, who possibly could? Jesus then stated that all things are possible with God (see v. 26).

Jesus knew there is no one at all who is righteous. No one can be saved by acts of goodness, for no one is good enough to get to heaven. That's why Jesus had to come and die for us. (See Rom. 3:10,12; 5:6-8.) And that's why a person centered on God and His Son is wise.

Unrighteousness Causes Problems

Ecclesiastes 7:20, which states that there is not a righteous man on earth, begins a new section and a new thought. The new thought is this: Sin destroys relationships. It wrecked our relationship with God, it ruins our relationship with our families, friends and acquaintances and it alienates the sexes. Since no one could possibly find meaning cast alone in the universe, sin—if it had no cure—would have dashed all hope for meaning.

Because of sin in the Garden of Eden, there is spiritual death through separation from God (see Rom. 5:12). There is no righteous one on earth, the Teacher said. And he was right. We are all in need of Jesus' life-giving salvation.

*Do not pay attention to every word
        people say,
    or you may hear your servant
        cursing you—
for you know in your heart*

> *that many times you yourself have*
> *cursed others.*
> Ecclesiastes 7:21,22

These two verses show what our sinful natures can do to our relationships with those around us. Because he was talking to rulers, Solomon speaks of servants. But the main idea relates to any human relationship. While we all try to be at peace with those around us, it is a fact that on all levels of human relationships—family, friends, outsiders, nations and races—we see constant examples of strife and conflict.

The Teacher again states the hopelessness of trying to find wisdom apart from the basis of it—centering on God:

> *All this I tested by wisdom and I said,*
> *"I am determined to be wise"—*
> *but this was beyond me.*
> *Whatever wisdom may be,*
> *it is far off and most profound—*
> *who can discover it?*
> *So I turned my mind to understand,*
> *to investigate and to search out*
> *wisdom and the scheme of*
> *things*
> *and to understand the stupidity of*
> *wickedness*
> *and the madness of folly.*
> Ecclesiastes 7:23-25

He spoke of the uselessness of those who try to take comfort in immoral relationships:

> *I find more bitter than death*
> *the woman who is a snare,*
> *whose heart is a trap*
> *and whose hands are chains.*

> *The man who pleases God will escape*
>> *her,*
>> *but the sinner she will ensnare.*
>> Ecclesiastes 7:26

There is a wider meaning to this verse than the mere physical act of sex with a prostitute. Solomon, like so many before and after him, had prostituted his beliefs. He sold out. He went after something he knew to be wrong, in the vain hope he could find some measure of fulfillment beyond God. Sin never fulfills.

> *"Look," says the Teacher, "this is*
> *what I have discovered:*
> *"Adding one thing to another to*
>> *discover the scheme of*
>> *things—*
> *while I was still searching*
> *but not finding—*
> *I found one upright man among a*
>> *thousand,*
> *but not one upright woman among*
>> *them all."*
>> Ecclesiastes 7:27,28

Of a thousand men in his employ, Solomon found one that seemed half acceptable. The other 999 were disappointments. His thousand wives and concubines (see 1 Kings 11:3) were apparently not real hot in the faithfulness department. This verse is undoubtedly an exaggerated—even humorous—view of reality to help make a serious point. Sin has loused up humanity's hopes of finding meaning. Even relationships as close as a man and woman can enjoy provide no guarantee of happiness.

Only God can heal the damage done by sin. Solomon seems to recognize this fact when he admits, "This only have I found: God made mankind upright, but men have gone in search of many schemes" (Eccles. 7:29).

1. Why do you suppose people sometimes act as though they can create a better life for themselves than God can?

2. Read Matthew 23, in which Jesus castigates the Pharisees. Just for fun, create an imaginary rock band called the "Fair I Sees." Give each member of the band—there are many—a name or nickname that corresponds to one of the criticisms Jesus leveled at the Pharisees.

   What lessons from Matthew 23 can you apply to your own life and relationship with the Lord?

3. Look at the list of ideas a high school student could use to help gain wisdom. Which ideas have you tried?

   Which ones do you need to work on?

   Can you think of any additional good ideas?

4. Read James 1:5-8. How does James say to get wisdom?

   In what ways does the passage correlate with Ecclesiastes 7? In what ways does it differ?

5. Imagine that in response to Ecclesiastes 7:16-18 you are trying to avoid slavish legalism or too "libbed" libertarianism in your Christian life. Take a few minutes to list things that you would have to avoid.

   Have you ever met anyone too extreme in his or her beliefs?

   How can you keep your devotion to God accurately centered on Him?

6. Think of your involvement with family, friends and those in authority over you (teachers or bosses) this past week.

   In what ways, if any, do you think sin has negatively influenced your relationships?

   In what ways, if any, has your Christianity had a positive influence?

   What simple things could you do to improve?

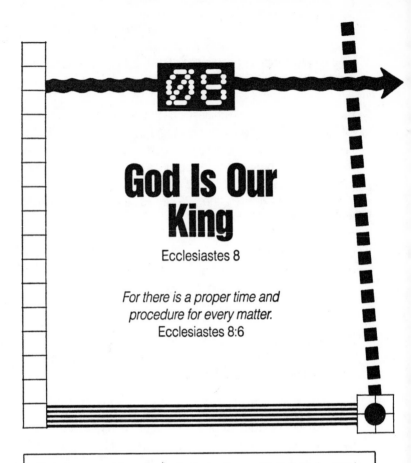

God Is Our King

Ecclesiastes 8

*For there is a proper time and
procedure for every matter.*
Ecclesiastes 8:6

Christians must be wise in their dealings with those who are in
positions of authority.

When the queen of Sheba saw the wisdom of Solomon, as well
as the palace he had built, the food on his table, the seating of his
officials, the attending servants in their robes, the cupbearers in
their robes and the burnt offerings he made at the temple of the
Lord, she was overwhelmed." 2 Chronicles 9:3,4

The queen of Sheba wasn't exactly poor, you know. She arrived with "a very great caravan—with camels carrying spices, large quantities of gold, and precious stones" (2 Chron. 9:1). Still, she was knocked out by Solomon's operation.

At first, she was probably quite impressed with her own wealth and power. Her caravan was undoubtedly designed to instill awe and envy in the eyes of the common people along the 1,200 miles of her trip from Africa. "Ah, groveling—I love it!" she may have said. But as she pulled into Jerusalem and wound up the hill toward the palace, we can imagine the nature of the emotions that began to play inside her. She was stunned by what Solomon had built. The palace was magnificent. The Temple, at the highest elevation, was a true wonder of the ancient world. Then, inside the palace, face-to-face with the king at last, she was literally overwhelmed by the pomp and circumstance of the court, the achievements of his wisdom and the wealth and ritualism displayed even in the religious sacrifices made at the fabulously ornate Temple.

She most likely was not the first of all royal visitors to ask, "How have you done this?"

It's safe to assume that she and many other thunderstruck guests told Solomon that they wished to return home to emulate, even in some small fashion, the elegance and magnificence of his court.

Ecclesiastes 8 seems to be a sort of *Solomon's Book of Royal Etiquette*. It is really an operator's manual describing the way a decent kingdom should be run. In it, Solomon lists the proper way both rulers and subjects should be expected to behave. The chapter seems to be Solomon's advice to those who wanted to run their little empires the way he ran his.

Who's in Charge Here?

There is a sense in which we as individuals have our own little "empires." We each have a small but real amount of influence over those around us. Therefore, we have duties and responsibilities much as a king would have. As we study Ecclesiastes 8, we can apply what we read to our personal behavior. You'll find it to be a practical chapter with lots of good advice for conducting your own domain—even if you're a high school sophomore instead of his highness, Solomon.

But before Solomon got into his advice for rulers and rulees he offered, by way of introduction, another worthwhile comment on wisdom:

Who is like the wise man?
Who knows the explanation of
        things?
Wisdom brightens a man's face
    and changes its hard appearance.
        Ecclesiastes 8:1

None of us know what is really going on in this world. We don't even know what *we* are doing half the time, much less what God is doing. But we do know that God is in charge. He holds the explanation of things. The wise person will forget about trying to know everything and will concentrate on knowing God.

Psalm 34:5 says, "Those who look to him are radiant; their faces are never covered with shame." Those who wisely look to God will find success as they conduct their lives, whether they be in authority as king or under authority as subject. Their faces will reflect their joy.

Now let's look at Solomon's list of rules for subjects to live by. Use your Bible to refer to the complete wording of the verses not quoted in full.

Rules for Subjects

1. Obey those in authority.
Ecclesiastes 8:2 begins the list with the obvious:

Obey the king's command, I say, because you took an oath before God.

The verse specifically refers to someone who officially serves in the king's employ, but it certainly applies even to those of us under the authority of a parent, school teacher or boss. In our case, our commitment to Jesus constitutes our oath before God and therefore requires our obedience to those God has put in authority over us.

Romans 13:1-7 has the final word on this rule. It explains that everyone must submit to governing authorities because God is the one who allows them authority. Anyone who rebels against authority good or bad is thus rebelling against what God has instituted. Those who obey will have no need to fear those in charge.

The fact that we have made a commitment to Christ and that God has set up the authorities brings up an important point. We obey people because we obey God.´ Our allegiance is to God. While there are times when we must disobey people (we'll talk about that later), there never comes a time when we can justifiably disobey our Master.

We see in these passages a sort of test by which we can measure our level of obedience and commitment to God. If we tend to be rebellious to parents, teachers and bosses, then our commitment to God is at low ebb and needs work.

If our attitude is one of godly submission to authority—even when it is inconvenient—this indicates our commitment to God is probably quite healthy.

Jesus told a tale that applies to this discussion:

"What do you think? There was a man who had two sons. He went to the first and said, 'Son, go and work today in the vineyard.'

"'I will not,' he answered, but later he changed his mind and went.

"Then the father went to the other son and said the same thing. He answered, 'I will, sir,' but he did not go.

"Which of the two did what his father wanted?"
Matthew 21:28-31

The first one did his father's will. He didn't want to in the beginning, but he obeyed. The second son promised to obey, but did not. The mature Christian will do the Lord's will even when it means obeying seemingly unreasonable demands from parents, teachers or bosses. The weak Christian may have promised to follow and obey Jesus, but washes out when the water gets a little deep.

2. Don't immediately bail out on a leader with whom you disagree.
Do not be in a hurry to leave the king's presence. Do not stand up for a bad cause, for he will do whatever he pleases.
Ecclesiastes 8:3

Rule Two is a great suggestion to keep in mind when you have ridden into mortal combat against your mom or dad. If you are angry or hurt, don't just storm out the door. Stay. Try to come to some meeting of the minds. It's not always easy but it is the wise thing to do. As Jesus promised, "Blessed are the peacemakers, for they will be called sons of God" (Matt. 5:9).

3. Don't haggle over unimportant things.
Rule Three is also based on Ecclesiastes 8:3. If you must disagree with your parents, don't do it over little things. Cultivate a strong friendship with your folks. That way, they will perhaps be more willing to listen to you when you feel you have a legitimate problem. In the end, whether or not they decide to do what you want, the decision is up to them.

4. Recognize and submit to authority unless . . .
Since a king's word is supreme, who can say to him, "What are you doing?" Ecclesiastes 8:4

Only God can question the king. Romans 13:1-7 makes it clear that only on very rare occasions will God allow us to question authority. However, it does happen.

Daniel refused to obey a new law requiring that all prayer be directed to the Babylonian king (see Daniel 6). And, when ordered by the Sadducees to stop preaching about Jesus, Peter replied, "We must obey God rather than men" (Acts 5:29). In both cases the people who stood against the authorities were severely punished.

Daniel was thrown into the lions' den and the high priest and his associates ordered Peter and the apostles with him to be flogged (beaten). Happily, Daniel was saved from the hungry lions, and Peter and his companions rejoiced in suffering for Jesus' sake.

In high school, a friend of mine had a Mormon teacher for his English class. One day she claimed that, "The Bible says that black people are inferior to white people."

Now understand; this was in the 1960s, a time of deep unrest between the races. To say a thing like that was not only stupid and bigoted, is was dangerously provocative. I don't know how the other students reacted, but my friend Rick—a white man—stood up and said, "Where?"

The teacher said "'Where,' what?" Rick said, "Where in the Bible does it say black people are inferior?" The teacher blushed and claimed that she couldn't show him right then because she didn't have her Bible.

"Here," said Rick, "take mine." He held up the Bible he always carried. Obviously the teacher was unable to find such a passage.

End of argument.

Rick took a stand for truth. He had to stand up to an evil teacher to do it. There are times when we must go against authority, but always be prepared for the consequences and be sure you have the Bible on your side.

5. Hold your mug until the proper time.

*Whoever obeys his command will come
   to no harm,
   and the wise heart will know the
      proper time and procedure.
For there is a proper time and
      procedure for every matter,
   though a man's misery weighs
      heavily upon him.*
   Ecclesiastes 8:5,6

Even if you are deeply troubled and feel a need to change the mind of one in authority, there are times when you just need to keep quiet. A wise person knows when to be a squeaky wheel and when to steer clear. This is called having tact and diplomacy.

I once worked in the maintenance department of a high rise office building. I liked my immediate supervisor very much, a strong man of good character. But whenever I worked with him, he swore constantly. For some reason, swearing has always particularly bugged me. I hate it. I wanted to talk to him about it, but he was my boss. Besides, I was just a kid and so why would he respect anything I said?

One day he found out I was a Christian. He started telling me about his daughter, also a Christian. I asked him if he ever went to church with her and he said, sure, he went with her all the time. "I'm a Christian," he said.

I saw my opening, so I got up my nerve, pulled my pants up to my armpits and said, "Jay, if you are a Christian, how come you cuss so much?"

Now, I immediately realized that was a stupid, undiplomatic thing to say. But it basically communicated my intent so I let it stand.

Jay looked squarely at me, mouth hanging open, as if I'd just hit him in the face. I could hear my paychecks coming to a screeching halt.

Jay confessed that it had never occurred to him that he should live the same upright life at work that he lived at church. There was a definite and obvious change in his behavior from that moment on.

Unknowingly, I had followed the Teacher's advice. I had waited for the proper time to correct one in authority over me.

6. Remember, the king isn't perfect.
Since no man knows the future,
who can tell him what is to come?
No man has power over the wind to
contain it;
so no one has power over the day of
his death.
As no one is discharged in time of war,

so wickedness will not release those
    who practice it.
    Ecclesiastes 8:7,8

The basic point is that the king has limits on his power. No one in authority can know all there is to know, make everything turn out all right (or all wrong) or escape the inevitable results of his or her own evil leadership. Practically, this means that no leader should be placed high on a pedestal or thought of as a "savior of the nation." Hopefully, our leaders are the best they can be, but no one can expect them to completely put right what years of foolish leadership has put wrong. On a level closer to home, we must always realize that our parents deserve some slack. Allow them to make a few mistakes. Also there is justice in the end for the wicked. God will see to that.

Rules for Kings
Here are some solid suggestions for the attitudes and behavior you should display in running your "kingdom."

1. Pride hurts you.
In Ecclesiastes 8:9, Solomon reports that people in authority lord it over others to their own detriment. In Proverbs 8:13, God says, "I hate pride and arrogance, evil behavior and perverse speech." The person who thinks he or she is superior to others is in big trouble with the Lord.

2. You won't get away with anything.
Then too, I saw the wicked buried—those who used to come and go from the holy place and receive praise in the city where they did this. This too is meaningless.
    Ecclesiastes 8:10

Solomon saw evil rulers praised in their lifetime and buried with respect. It was meaningless to him, for they didn't deserve it. But the thing to remember is this: Even if they were buried in respect, they are still dead. "Man is destined to die once, and after that to face judgment" (Heb. 9:27). They have a divine appointment with God to answer for their crimes and unjust actions.

3. Carry out justice quickly.
Ecclesiastes 8:11 reveals the results of delayed justice: higher crime rates.

You do a big favor to someone when you correct them for their wrongdoings. If you shy away and hope the problem resolves itself, you have done them a disservice.

4. Do the right thing, avoid the wrong things.
In Ecclesiastes 8:12,13, Solomon said that although he has seen exceptions to the rule, it's usually true that God-fearing people have fewer problems than wicked people. We know that in the end, when God steps in, there will be no exceptions to the rule.

Each of us has a sphere of influence, a circle of people that we can affect either positively or negatively. If we wish to be a positive force, we must live and behave uprightly. This is especially so if we want to be examples of what Christ can do.

5. Reward righteousness, punish wickedness.
The wise leader rewards the righteous and punishes the wicked. To do the opposite is a common meaningless injustice (see Eccles. 8:14). Politicians sometimes try to make deals with crooks and dishonest power brokers. In essence, this is rewarding evil.

We are rewarding evil when we laugh at cruel gossip, agree with mean comments about others or drool with a friend over the less-than-tasteful end of the magazine rack.

Rewarding good is what we do when we pay a compliment, appreciate a favor, offer to help or invite another to join in a positive activity.

King of Kings
Here are some words to describe the sort of person you should strive to be: obedient, loyal, amiable, easy to get along with, diplo-

matic, accepting, other-centered instead of pridefully self-centered, aware that evil does not go unpunished, righteous, a positive influence, appreciative. See if you can find these traits spelled out or hinted at in the preceding five rules.

If you are this sort of person, you should have little difficulty following Solomon's next recommendation:

> *So I commend the enjoyment of life, because nothing is better for a man under the sun than to eat and drink and be glad. Then joy will accompany him in his work all the days of the life God has given him under the sun.*
>
> *When I applied my mind to know wisdom and to observe man's labor on earth—his eyes not seeing sleep day or night—then I saw all that God has done. No one can comprehend what goes on under the sun. Despite all his efforts to search it out, man cannot discover its meaning. Even if a wise man claims he knows, he cannot really comprehend it.*
> Ecclesiastes 8:15-17

The king in Jerusalem ends his advice to the kings of the earth by tipping his crown to the King of kings. Only God can do what He does, it's too great for even the wisest man on earth to understand. Therefore, enjoy the life God has given you—knowing you will not always understand, but accepting that God has your best interest in mind.

1. Who are the people in your sphere of influence? In what ways could observing Solomon's suggestions affect them positively?

2. Earlier in this chapter, I stated that if we tend to be rebellious to parents, teachers and bosses, then our commitment to God is at low ebb and needs work. If our attitude is one of godly submission to authority—even when it is inconvenient—this indicates our commitment to God is probably quite healthy. Examine your attitude towards those in authority over you (parents, teachers,

employers, coach). In each case, rate how well you think you are doing in submitting to their authority.

What are some specific steps you could take to do better?

3. Read Psalm 73. The author was frustrated—as was Solomon—over the way wicked people prospered. What event occurred in verse 17 that changed the author's attitude?

Memorize Psalm 73:28.

4. What methods does your family use to resolve disagreements and conflicts?

Are the methods effective?

What part do you play in helping reach a satisfactory resolution?

In what ways could you be a better peacemaker?

5. Have you ever felt that you've been ordered to do something against God's will? What did you do?

6. On a piece of paper, write in your own words what the following verses tell you about pride: Psalm 10:2; 73:4-7; Proverbs 8:13; 13:10; 16:18,19; 29:23; Mark 7:14-23; 1 John 2:16.

7. Ecclesiastes 8:15 says in part: "Then joy will accompany him in his work all the days of the life God has given him under the sun." When Solomon mentions work, he is talking about a job and all the other things a person must do to stay alive. A Christian also has a "job"—it is to do the will of God. Make a list of at least ten things you feel God wants you to do, not just in the future but today.

Also make a list of at least ten character traits God wants you to display.

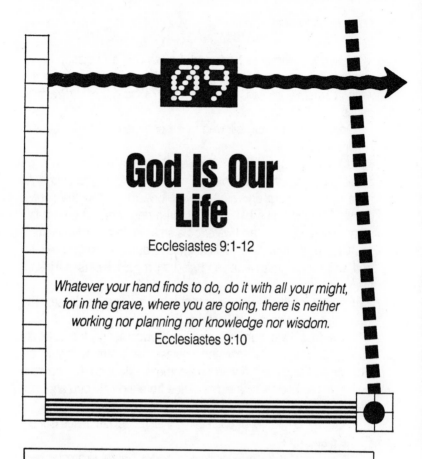

God Is Our Life

Ecclesiastes 9:1-12

*Whatever your hand finds to do, do it with all your might,
for in the grave, where you are going, there is neither
working nor planning nor knowledge nor wisdom.*
Ecclesiastes 9:10

The common destiny awaiting all people is physical death. Facing this fact causes people to consider how they should live.

Live, from Studio C in Hollywood, it's the *Heraldo Rutabaga Show!*"

[Wildly enthusiastic applause]

The opening fanfare is cued and the television camera pans across the cheering audience. There, in the middle of the crowd, stands the man himself, Heraldo Rutabaga, well-known semiliterate talk show host.

Heraldo, flashing his trademark boyish grin and staring knowingly into the lens—then turning around when he realizes he has the wrong camera—intones, "Life. What is it? Who gets it?" (Dramatic pause) "We'll be right back."

Opening credits roll, followed by six commercials for things with lemons in them.

"All right, we are back. I'm Heraldo Rutabaga and with me in the studio today are three people I'm sure you're going to enjoy." All eyes follow camera one as it moves forward to view the show's guests who are seated in a row of three desk chairs up on a low stage. There is coffee and water on a small table in front of them.

"On the left, from Ancient Israel, we've dug up a man known far and wide for his great wealth and wisdom, my close personal friend, the Teacher!"

Heraldo pretends to be interrupted by the applause. The Teacher, old, waves a bony hand at the world.

"Seated on the right is a relative newcomer to the celebrity scene. Ladies and gentlemen, please—a warm welcome for Nobody N. Particular!" A warm welcome is extended. Nobody, the guest, smiles and takes a sip of coffee from a dainty cup and saucer.

"And in the middle, of course you'll all recognize Jesus Christ." (Polite clapping.)

"We all want to know what life is all about," Heraldo pronounces. "We've all asked *the* Big Question: 'Why am I here?' Good question, ladies and gentlemen. Why *are* we here? Teacher, let's start with you. Why aren't we over there?"

"What?"

"Just joking! Ha, Ha. But seriously, can you tell us what life is all about?"

What's Life?

If we really could interview the Teacher, the Lord and Nobody N. Particular (the typical person on the street) we might ask them to tell us their thoughts about the meaning of life. The following is what we might be told.

The Teacher

Life is a confusing knot. I've had the best of it—power, position, wealth, women, food and drink yet I found all these things to be empty. Meaningless. Events come as they come, get me down or lift me up. Some make me sad, some make me happy. There seems to be no meaning to it apart from God. Only God knows what's going on.

Nobody N. Particular

Life is a confusing knot. I wish I had the good life—power, position, wealth, women, food and drink—but I'm too poor and ugly. Events come as they come, get me down or lift me up. Some make me sad, some make me happy. There seems to be no meaning to it. If there is a God, maybe He knows what's going on.

The Lord

"I am the way and the truth and the life" (John 14:6). "I have come that they may have life, and have it to the full" (John 10:10). "I am the vine; you are the branches. If a man remains in me and I in him, he will bear much fruit; apart from me you can do nothing. I have told you this so that my joy may be in you and that your joy may be complete" (John 15:5,11).

The View from the Grave

So I reflected on all this and concluded that the righteous and the wise and what they do are in God's hands, but no man knows whether love or hate awaits him. All share a common destiny—the righteous and the wicked, the good and the bad, the clean and the unclean, those who offer sacrifices and those who do not.

> *As it is with the good man,*
> > *so with the sinner,*
> *as it is with those who take oaths,*
> > *so with those who are afraid to take*
> > > *them.*

This is the evil in everything that happens under the sun:

The same destiny overtakes all. The hearts of men, moreover, are full of evil and there is madness in their hearts while they live, and afterward they join the dead. Ecclesiastes 9:1-3

Throughout Ecclesiastes the Teacher has asked one question over and over: "Why do good people sometimes suffer while wicked people are blessed?" In these first verses of chapter nine, he summed up his frustration by proclaiming that what a person believes or how he or she behaves has nothing to do with what life has in store. The good person, the wise, the righteous, the wicked, the healthy, the sick, the religious, the atheist, the active, the uninvolved and the unrepentant sinner—the Teacher condemns them all to the same shallow grave called death. In life, love awaits some and hate awaits others—only God knows who will receive one or the other—but death unites all.

The Teacher seems to be calling attention to something that many have observed and been troubled by: the injustice, the wacky disorder of life and the unpredictable nature of events. If God is in control, why do things seem so very much out of control? (See also Eccles. 3:11, 6:1,2,12; 7:13,14; 8:14,17.)

He struggled to resolve this problem and came up with this position: "God is in control, but we can't figure out what He's up to. All we can do is trust Him and be content. Apart from God, nothing makes sense." That is why the Teacher said, "Meaningless! Meaningless! Utterly Meaningless! Everything is meaningless" (see Eccles. 1:2).

You and I have a tremendous advantage over the Teacher. Jesus has revealed so much to us. Jesus said, "Everything that I learned from my Father I have made known to you" (John 15:15.) John 1:1 speaks of Jesus as the Word. It says, "In the beginning was the Word, and the Word was with God, and the Word was God." Verse 14 says, "The Word became flesh and made his dwelling among us. We have seen his glory, the glory of the One and Only, who came from the Father, full of grace and truth." God became man. His nature and truth has been recorded for us in the New Testament, a treasure which the Teacher never owned. We know much more about the nature of God and about what God wants us to do than wise old Solomon ever did.

Solomon had much more limited insight into the afterlife than we can have. We can face the next world not only with calm and confidence but also with great anticipation. This is truly good news for Christians.

A basic journalism principle is that a good news story will always supply the answers to these five inquiries: Who? What? When? Where? and Why? Regarding death, the Teacher could only answer one of these questions. He didn't know *where* or *when* death would occur for himself or anyone else. He didn't know *what* would happen when death did occur—though he took a stab at the question (see Eccles. 9:5,10). He certainly had no answer for the *why* behind life and death, it was all meaningless to him. The only one he had a solid answer for is *who*: us.

As Christians, in possession of better facts, we can supply better answers. Although we still don't know *where* or *when* (which is certainly God's wisdom at work) we do have a much improved picture of *what* will happen after death. As Paul said, "For to me, to live is Christ and to die is gain . . . . I desire to depart and be with Christ, which is better by far" (Phil. 1:21,23).

As for *why* things happen as they do, we are finite and cannot hope to know everything perfectly, but we do have a broader base of understanding than Solomon. We know, for instance, that "it is God who works in you to will and to act according to his good purpose" (Phil. 2:13). And we know that "the testing of your faith develops perseverance. Perseverance must finish its work so that you may be mature and complete, not lacking anything" (James 1:3,4).

Now as for the *who* involved in death. The teacher said "us." But we can say "Us and God." God does not desert us at the cemetery. There are far too many comforting verses to quote, but here is a sampling: Jesus, speaking to a repentant criminal being crucified at His side, said, "I tell you the truth, today you will be with me in paradise" (Luke 23:43). Romans 14:8 is a great one to memorize: "If we live, we live to the Lord; and if we die, we die to the Lord. So, whether we live or die, we belong to the Lord." Here is a wonderful promise: "All things are yours, whether . . . the world or life or death or the present or the future—all are yours, and you are of Christ, and Christ is of God" (1 Cor. 3:21-23). If you want to have your socks peeled back, read 1 Corinthians 15:12-58.

To a child of the living God, death is the final severing of any meaninglessness. It allows the full experience of life eternal.

Hope in God

Anyone who is among the living has hope—even a live dog is better off than a dead lion!

For the living know that they will die,
but the dead know nothing;
they have no further reward,
and even the memory of them is
forgotten.
Their love, their hate
and their jealousy have long since
vanished;
never again will they have a part
in anything that happens under the
sun.
Ecclesiastes 9:4-6

Solomon was trying to paint a picture of what life on earth is like if there is no God of life to whom we can turn. If there is no God to hope in, then our only hope is to stumble upon a little bit of meaning and purpose while we are yet alive. Death is the end of all hope.

But our hope is Christ. To refute some people who claimed to believe in Christ but not in the resurrection of the dead, Paul wrote:

If there is no resurrection of the dead, then not even Christ has been raised. And if Christ has not been raised, our preaching is useless and so is your faith . . . . And if Christ has not been raised, your faith is futile; you are still in your sins. Then those who have fallen asleep in Christ are lost. If only for this life we

have hope in Christ, we are to be pitied more than all men.
1 Corinthians 15:13,14,17-19

Notice the difference between the Teacher's view of death and Paul's. For the Christian, Paul called it sleep. That's not to say that those now dead in Christ wait in the grave until some future day. It means that those of us still alive will one day see our departed Christian brothers and sisters, like the dawning of a new day.

Paul, ever the expert of things spiritual, also had this to say about hope:

> *Therefore, since we have been justified through faith, we have peace with God through our Lord Jesus Christ, through whom we have gained access by faith into this grace in which we now stand. And we rejoice in the hope of the glory of God. Not only so, but we also rejoice in our sufferings, because we know that suffering produces perseverance; perseverance, character; and character, hope. And hope does not disappoint us, because God has poured out his love into our hearts by the Holy Spirit, whom he has given us.* Romans 5:1-5

There are three thoughts about hope in this passage: The Christian's joyful hope is fulfilled in the glory of God (we'll be like Jesus in that we'll share many of His character traits; see 1 John 3:2); the proven character built by suffering gives us hope (because it gives us a taste of His quality of character; see 1 Pet. 4:1,2); our future destiny is assured because He lovingly gave us the Holy Spirit to make the changes in us (see 1 Cor. 2:10-12; Gal. 5:22,23). This passage helps to answer the Teacher's questions about why things happen as they do. Bad things are allowed to come so that we can become more like Him.

According to the worldly viewpoint, spoken of by the Teacher, the dead are out of it. To this way of thinking, the only reasonable thing a person could do, then, is this:

Go, eat your food with gladness, and drink your wine with a

joyful heart, for it is now that God favors what you do. Always be clothed in white, and always anoint your head with oil. Enjoy life with your wife, whom you love, all the days of this meaningless life that God has given you under the sun—all your meaningless days. Whatever your hand finds to do, do it with all your might, for in the grave, where you are going, there is neither working nor planning nor knowledge nor wisdom.
Ecclesiastes 9:7-10

Party hearty, mates, for this is it. This brings up a fascinating consideration. The Teacher says to have fun while you can because the grim reaper is breathing down your neck. But Paul says that to live like Christ and to die is better than hanging around (see Phil. 1:21,23). Can they both be right? To the average non-Christian, Paul's teaching sounds absurd! To the Christians who understand Jesus' promises, the Teacher's wisdom may not at first sound so wise.

This is a classic example of how Jesus can heal and transform a person's character traits. If you know the Lord, you know exactly what Paul is talking about. If you don't know the Lord, what He says couldn't possibly have any appeal.

Actually, the Teacher and Paul are closer to each other in what they said than it might seem. The Teacher is not really advocating a wild, thrill-a-minute life-style. He's just saying once again that if you don't center your life on God you may as well try to enjoy what you do and forget the bad news at the end of the trail. For the worldly, that's all there is. Paul, on the other hand, never says that Christians can't have any fun. They both want to enjoy life. But Paul knows there is no end of the trail for the Christian.

I have seen something else under the sun:
The race is not to the swift
or the battle to the strong,
nor does food come to the wise
or wealth to the brilliant
or favor to the learned;

but time and chance happen to them
  all.
Moreover, no man knows when his hour will come:
As fish are caught in a cruel net,
  or birds are taken in a snare,
so men are trapped by evil times
  that fall unexpectedly upon them.
  Ecclesiastes 9:11,12

Speed, strength, wisdom, intellect, skill—none of these things guarantee happiness in life. Time and chance destroys that hope. Nobody can escape the roll of the dice.

This passage, indeed this whole chapter, has shown that apart from God death is a trap from which no one escapes. But for the Christian, death ushers in a state of true freedom. Freedom to finally enjoy all the promises, all the pleasures, all the gifts that this world seems to offer but forever withholds.

What's It Gonna Be?

If Ecclesiastes 9 isn't a call to switch from a worldly philosophy to God's truth, what is it?!

Here's what the world has to offer us: everybody ends up stuck in the ground; the good people have no advantage whatever; death will destroy any hope we have; our lives are without meaning; there is no joy in the grave; time and chance will wreak our best plans and dreams; the net of death will bring everything to a useless, senseless close. Wow.

And what does Jesus have to offer? In this life He offers peace, hope, and meaning. After death He offers eternal life, total fulfillment, never ending joy, fabulous heavenly wealth, the unexpected adventures that heaven will bring, true love.

Read the encouraging words Paul wrote in his letter to the church at Thessalonica:

"Brothers, we do not want you to be ignorant about those who fall asleep, or to grieve like the rest of men, who have no

hope. We believe that Jesus died and rose again and so we believe that God will bring with Jesus those who have fallen asleep in him. According to the Lord's own word, we tell you that we who are still alive, who are left till the coming of the Lord, will certainly not precede those who have fallen asleep. For the Lord himself will come down from heaven, with a loud command, with the voice of the archangel and with the trumpet call of God, and the dead in Christ will rise first. After that, we who are still alive and are left will be caught up with them in the clouds to meet the Lord in the air. And so we will be with the Lord forever. Therefore encourage each other with these words. 1 Thessalonians 4:13-18

1. Do you know people who believe in God but seem to be confused about life or are living ungodly lives?

   If such a friend came to you and in all seriousness asked about the meaning of life, how would you respond?

2. Look up the following passages to learn more about death, judgment and life after death. Matthew 25:31-34; Luke 16:19-31; 20:34-36; John 14:1-4; 2 Corinthians 12:2-4; Colossians 3:1-4; 2 Peter 3:1-13; Revelation 2:7; 21:1-8; 22:1-6.

3. We've pointed out some of the positive aspects of physical death, such as the opportunity it provides to enter a better world. Obviously, death has many sad aspects to it. Make a list of at least five positive aspects of a Christian's death, and a few sad aspects.

   If death provides a better world for the Christian, what purpose does God give to our life on earth? (See Matt. 24:14; 28:16-20.)

4. Paraphrase Romans 5:1-5.

   If you like crosswords, you might like this challenge: Using as many of the significant words as you can from Romans 5:1-5, create a crossword puzzle for someone else to solve. Keep refining the puzzle until all the words are tightly intertwined. Write good clues and have fun!

5. Paul's emphasis on eternity does not mean that it is wrong to have good, clean fun in this life. What are some of the fun activities that you think are appropriate for a Christian to enjoy?

What are some that you would reject?

Which fun ones do you participate in?

Is it possible for these good things, if mishandled, to somehow interfere with your relationship with God?

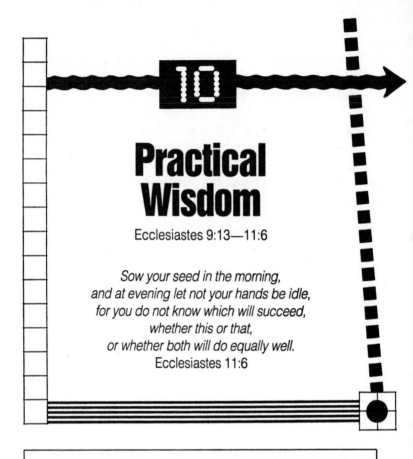

10

Practical Wisdom

Ecclesiastes 9:13—11:6

*Sow your seed in the morning,
and at evening let not your hands be idle,
for you do not know which will succeed,
whether this or that,
or whether both will do equally well.*
Ecclesiastes 11:6

God honors those Christians who use His wisdom to direct their activities.

Time for the Acme Wisdom Quotient Examination. Get out your pencil and circle the appropriate answers:

1. You're driving your car when suddenly a pedestrian looms in front of you. What would you do?

   a. Lay on the horn, speed up and run the clod over.

   b. Cover your eyes with both hands and scream.
   c. Slow down and stop.

2. You owe the heavyweight boxing champion of the world one thousand dollars. What would you do?

   a. Get whole-body medical insurance.
   b. Take boxing lessons and wear a suit of armor.
   c. Pay up.

3. You've just learned about the law of gravity in school. What would you do?
   a. Jump off the World Trade Center to test the law.
   b. Try to join the Gravity Police to help uphold the law.
   c. Remember it next time you walk along the edge of a cliff.

4. You want to be thought of as a wise person. What would you do?

   a. Take drugs, drop out of school, throw rocks at passing police cars and play solitaire Russian roulette until you win.
   b. Eat fish 'cause everybody knows it's brain food.
   c. Go to God, the source of wisdom.

If you answered anything but *c* for each question, you better check your house for radon emissions.

True wisdom is a combination of two things: wise thinking and wise behavior. A person who knows the right thing to do but doesn't do it is a fool. We all know smoking is idiotic, but many people suck cigarettes. Likewise, the person who doesn't know what to do but happens to stumble upon the right move reaps the reward of his or her good fortune. (This is often called "beginner's luck.")

The Bible contains a great deal of wisdom. It shows how to think wisely and live wisely. Those who listen to God's words and put them into practice are like the wise man who built his house on the rock. Those who reject His words will wash out with the next high tide (see Matt. 7:24-27). The Ecclesiastes passage we are now going to examine is a list of suggestions for wise thinking and wise living. As always, our study will include words of wisdom from other parts of the Bible. See which ones you habitually apply in your own thinking and behavior.

Wisdom's Reward

I also saw under the sun this example of wisdom that greatly impressed me: There once was a small city with only a few people in it. And a powerful king came against it, surrounded it and built huge siegeworks against it. Now there lived in that city a man poor but wise, and he saved the city by his wisdom. But nobody remembered that poor man. So I said, "Wisdom is better than strength." But the poor man's wisdom is despised, and his words are no longer heeded.
Ecclesiastes 9:13-16

The Teacher gives no further details in this little sketch. We don't know the city, the king or the wise man. We don't know what the wise man did that so influenced the outcome of events. But we do know that wisdom saved the lives of many and that the wise man was unrewarded and forgotten.

This is perhaps Solomon's way of asking us to consider the nature of wisdom's rewards. On one hand, the man saved his life and the lives of his neighbors. On the other, he stayed poor and was ignored.

A similar scenario is often played out in the world in a spiritual sense. A person wisely becomes a Christian—his or her life is saved from the devil's armies. The Christian leads others to Christ—their lives are saved through Jesus. Yet the Christian may not be honored or regarded by anyone except the Lord.

That's another story, however. Solomon noted that, while wisdom is often a great benefit, it is not a guarantee of worldly success. We've discussed this before. Some dreams will only be realized in heaven. Humility now, exaltation later. Try not to be disappointed, Solomon seems to be warning, if some acts of wisdom fail to achieve worldly success, do forget, "Time and chance happen to them all" (Eccles. 9:11). The motivation for exercising wisdom cannot be earthly reward, because reward is not always given. Instead, the motivation should come in knowing you are doing what is best.

Having extended this note of caution, the Teacher launches into a series of statements that describe the right things to do in various situations.

Ancient Proverbs for Modern Times

The quiet words of the wise are more to
> *be heeded*
than the shouts of a ruler of fools.
Wisdom is better than weapons of
> *war,*
> *but one sinner destroys much good.*
> Ecclesiastes 9:17,18

There are two main thoughts to this verse. One, whispered wisdom is better than shouted foolishness. Two, giving into sin will destroy the wise person.

Jesus gave some practical guidelines regarding the first:

"Be careful not to do your 'acts of righteousness' before men, to be seen by them. If you do, you will have no reward from your Father in heaven.

"So when you give to the needy, do not announce it with trumpets, as the hypocrites do in the synagogues and on the streets, to be honored by men. I tell you the truth, they have received their reward in full. But when you give to the needy, do not let your left hand know what your right hand is doing, so that your giving may be in secret. Then your Father, who sees what is done in secret, will reward you.

"And when you pray, do not be like the hypocrites, for they love to pray standing in the synagogues and on the street corners to be seen by men. I tell you the truth, they have received their reward in full. But when you pray, go into your room, close the door and pray to your Father, who is unseen. Then

> *your Father, who sees what is done in secret, will reward you.*
> *And when you pray, do not keep on babbling like pagans, for*
> *they think they will be heard because of their many words."*
> Matthew 6:1-7

Jesus also shed light on Ecclesiastes 9:18. About to address a huge crowd, He told His disciples, "Be on your guard against the yeast of the Pharisees, which is hypocrisy. There is nothing concealed that will not be disclosed, or hidden that will not be made known" (Luke 12:1,2). He compared the sin of hypocrisy to yeast. Just as a tiny amount of yeast will cause an entire loaf of bread to rise as it cooks, a seemingly small sin will make itself evident. Hypocrisy is a prime example, but the principle applies to all sin and to all sinners. No matter how wise and respected a person may be, sin will eventually topple the sinner. And, as the Teacher said, "one sinner destroys much good" (Eccles. 9:18).

This goes right along with the Teacher's next proverb:

> *As dead flies give perfume a bad*
> *   smell,*
> *so a little folly outweighs wisdom*
> *   and honor.*
> Ecclesiastes 10:1

This is an experiment you can do in the privacy of your own home. All you need is a fly swatter and your mom's best perfume. Of course, if you do try this, your mother will teach you exactly how far folly gets you.

> *The heart of the wise inclines to the*
> *   right,*
> *but the heart of the fool to the left.*
> *Even as he walks along the road,*
> *   the fool lacks sense*
> *   and shows everyone how stupid he is.*
> Ecclesiastes 10:2,3

Follow the road signs of life. The Bible is like a road map. It tells us where we are (lost in sin), where we should head (eternal life in Jesus) and how to get there (repentance, salvation and the rest).

Notice the progression of thought in the proverbs of Ecclesiastes 10:2,3: Heed the whispered words of wisdom; don't give in to a "little" sin, don't disregard these warnings or everyone will see how foolish you are.

Perhaps every youth group has examples of kids who simply refuse to live wisely. They hear the words of the Bible, but they don't heed them. They give in to temptation and become involved in some sin they think won't be found out. They ignore the advice and cautions extended by others and their own feelings of disquiet, if any. The results? The mildest result may be an ineffectual life for God; the worst is falling completely away from Him. In between there may be unwanted pregnancy, chemical dependence, severed friendships, hurt feelings, embarrassment, terrible illness and a whole lot more.

Who is the wise person? The one who chooses to turn God's way at the crossroads and then stays on the trail.

That's Not Fair!
Ecclesiastes 10:4-7 offers advice to those who are subjected to the whims of fools. Have you ever thought to yourself, "Maybe I got switched at the hospital. These people can't really be my parents!" Many people while growing up have to struggle with believing their parents have made unfair errors in judgment. Some people really do have folks who are truly awful. (That happens less often than kids claim and more often than adults admit.) Whatever the situation, this passage gives solid suggestions for coping with life when Mom and Dad aren't fair!

If a ruler's anger rises against you,
do not leave your post;
calmness can lay great errors to rest.
There is an evil I have seen under the
sun,

> *the sort of error that arises from a ruler:*
> *Fools are put in many high positions,*
>   *while the rich occupy the low ones.*
> *I have seen slaves on horseback,*
>   *while princes go on foot like slaves.*

Calmness is the key word here. When the swords have been drawn between you and your parents (or teacher or boss), a calm response is the only solution. Proverbs 15:1 puts it this way: "A gentle answer turns away wrath, but a harsh word stirs up anger." (Keep in mind Solomon's warning: Not every act of wisdom will be immediately rewarded. But God will keep accurate accounts and pay you back for your good efforts.)

Hopefully, you don't consider your parents to be enemies. But even if you do, a loving response is still the only one Scripture allows. "But love your enemies, do good to them." (Luke 6:35). And the apostle Peter wrote, "Above all, love each other deeply, because love covers over a multitude of sins" (1 Peter 4:8).

An important note: In the heat of anger, it is often impossible to *feel* love for the one who infuriates you. Even so, you can live up to these Bible verses by doing *acts* of love. That is, you can show kindness and obedience even if you don't want to. In the Bible, love is not an emotion. It is the Christian's way of life.

Think Ahead

One of the earmarks of wise thinking is the ability to foretell the negative consequences of foolish behavior. Mature people don't play on the freeway.

Ecclesiastes 10:8,9 mentions the word *may* four times. Each *may* is the center of a simple formula: Action *A* may lead to result *B*. Here are the four examples paraphrased:

If you dig a pit you may fall into it.
If you break into a snake den you may get bitten by a snake.
If you quarry stones you may get crushed.
If you split logs you may get splinters.

Seems simple enough, yes? But every day people fall into pits of their own making, get bitten by the results of sin and have their worlds cave in on them. It's as easy as falling off a log, and people do that too.

Please don't allow yourself to be wiped out by sin and foolishness. It is not worth it. Think ahead.

Ecclesiastes 10:10,11 gives additional hints of what happens when we don't think ahead:

If the ax is dull
*   and its edge unsharpened,*
more strength is needed
*   but skill will bring success.*
If a snake bites before it is charmed,
*   there is no profit for the charmer.*

It takes effort to live correctly, ten times more so if your skill is dulled by sin and foolishness. And if that sin and foolishness turns and bites you, you're not going to like the results.

A Fool from the Word "Go"

The Teacher keeps turning the screws on the fool. Ecclesiastes 10:12-14 describes the nature of the fool's mouth. Unlike the wise whose words are gracious (kind, polite, reverent), a fool's words are destructive. The Teacher describes the fool's words as "folly" and "wicked madness" (v. 13). This description could apply to gossip, lies, boasting, dirty jokes or hurtful statements. To make matters worse "The fool multiplies words" (v. 14). Not only does he talk foolishly, he also talks too much! Nobody can predict the future, but the fool has plenty of opinions about what's going to happen to whom and what a person should do to prepare for tomorrow (see v. 14).

Jesus must have been speaking to some very foolish people when He said to the Pharisees:

"You brood of vipers, how can you who are evil say anything
good? For out of the overflow of the heart the mouth speaks.

> *The good man brings good things out of the good stored up in him, and the evil man brings evil things out of the evil stored up in him. But I tell you that men will have to give account on the day of judgment for every careless word they have spoken. For by your words you will be acquitted, and by your words you will be condemned."* Matthew 12:34-37

It might be good to take a short break here to think about the power of words. When Jesus wanted to change the world, He didn't search for a thousand beautiful people. He didn't comb the land for the rich and famous. He wasn't interested in the educated. Twelve ordinary guys were what He needed. Men who could hear His words and then repeat them and build upon them. And Jesus has used these words in the process of changing this world. (See Heb. 4:12 for a classic description of the power of God's Word.)

A wise person, young or old, is one who learns how to effectively express his or her thoughts and feelings. A great deal can be accomplished by the spoken word.

More Good Stuff About the Fool

Lazy and incompetent. Those are the two charges laid at the feet of the fool in Ecclesiastes 10:15-18. The passage provides no letup in the Teacher's continuing indictment of the unwise.

"A fool's work wearies him; he does not know the way to town" (Eccles. 10:15). Yep, that's lazy and incompetent. If we were to squeeze a lesson out of this for our spiritual lives, it would be that a fool struggles and wastes energy trying to live life without God. And without God, he or she won't make it to the gates of the heavenly city.

The rest of the passage discusses the incompetence of unworthy and inexperienced leaders.

Ecclesiastes 10:19 attacks the "life is like a beer commercial" attitude: "A feast is made for laughter, and wine makes life merry, but money is the answer for everything." Fun, pleasure and 30-year mortgages are a part of life, but only a part.

A Christian friend recently observed, "You know, I just bought a new house. I've got a new baby. My wife and I have great jobs. Life is good. But something seems missing. I don't get it." Happily, he isn't a fool. It was easy for him to see that he had forgotten about someone named Jesus. After refocusing his life on the Lord, his outlook brightened greatly.

Ecclesiastes 10:20 cautions against unwise criticism of those in authority. Nobody likes a fool. Wise people don't like fools and fools don't like fools. The wise person, however, keeps quiet about it.

Practical Advice

Cast your bread upon the waters,
for after many days you will find it
again.
Ecclesiastes 11:1

The Teacher now begins a new train of thought. At first glimpse, verse 11:1 looks like the Teacher's train may have jumped the rails. Just what in the world is he talking about? Does he want us to toss our sandwiches in the bay, or what? Surely even in those hazy days of history people didn't dunk their donuts off the end of the dock. Who wants soggy bread?

No, the picture is one of planting grain at the edge of the river. Having a good supply of water, it will grow and then a good crop can be harvested and enjoyed. This is practical wisdom. The fool would eat the seed grain and then have nothing to work with. Instant gratification—a full stomach with no delay—is a fool's delight.

It takes time to do things right; time and planning. If you are interested in achieving your maximum potential in life, take time to plan how to get there. A few dead bugs can ruin your cologne, but a little time and planning will keep you smelling like a rose. If you do have a specific goal or dream that you would like to realize, try making a list of all the steps you would have to take to reach that goal and the things you would have to deny yourself in order to have the time and energy necessary to succeed.

Jesus said, "Suppose one of you wants to build a tower. Will he not first sit down and estimate the cost to see if he has enough money to complete it? For if he lays the foundation and is not able to finish it, everyone who sees it will ridicule him, saying 'This fellow began to build and was not able to finish'" (Luke 14:28-30).

In this passage, Jesus was advising the large crowds traveling with Him to count the cost of discipleship. Much time and planning is required to do a good job of following Him. Developing into a mature Christian does not happen instantly nor without effort, but the rewards are worth the effort.

"Give portions to seven, yes to eight, for you do not know what disaster may come upon the land" (Eccles. 11:2). Once you do begin to harvest your grain, the Teacher proclaims, share it generously. A person's life cannot have true meaning until it means something to other people.

This call to generosity comes with a hint: You may someday need to depend on the generosity of others. Solomon wrote in Proverbs 11:24-26:

> *One man gives freely, yet gains even*
> > *more;*
> > *another withholds unduly, but comes*
> > *to poverty.*
> *A generous man will prosper;*
> > *he who refreshes others will himself*
> > *be refreshed.*
> *People curse the man who hoards grain,*
> > *but blessing crowns him who is*
> > *willing to sell.*

Jesus said, "With the measure you use, it will be measured to you—and even more" (Mark 4:24). Paul wrote, "Each man should give what he has decided in his heart to give, not reluctantly or under compulsion, for God loves a cheerful giver" (2 Cor. 9:7).

Here's a passage that talks about being generous to *yourself*:

> *Do not be deceived: God cannot be mocked. A man reaps*
> *what he sows. The one who sows to please his sinful nature,*

from that nature will reap destruction; the one who sows to please the Spirit, from the Spirit will reap eternal life. Let us not become weary in doing good, for at the proper time we will reap a harvest if we do not give up. Galatians 6:7-9

This is a terrific promise to those of us who have decided to live according to Christ's commands. Paul has the optimism of one who knows the reward will come, if not now then in heaven.

Ecclesiastes 11:3-5 warns us not to try to draw a fine line with our planning. If planting grain, go ahead and plant it at the proper time—don't worry if the wind or clouds don't look quite right. Human wisdom is limited, we cannot guess the future. Trust in God.

"Sow your seed in the morning, and at evening let not your hands be idle, for you do not know which will succeed, whether this or that, or whether both will do equally well" (Eccles. 11:6). Work hard, whether you are an ancient high ruler or modern high schooler. The wise work hard. Conversely, it takes hard work to be wise. But don't worry, a little hard wisdom never hurt anybody.

1. Here are some synonyms for *wise*: judicious, rational, thoughtful, shrewd, prudent, astute, proper, discerning. Think about them and explain how they might relate to your behavior as a Christian.

2. The Bible contains a great deal of wisdom. It shows how to think wisely and live wisely. Those who listen to God's words and put them into practice are like the wise man who built his house on the rock (see Matt. 7:24-27). Pick a book of the Bible that you would like to read. Create a chart or calendar on which you have set aside a reasonable amount of time for daily study. As you read the book, write down any notes you want to keep and any questions you may have. Show the questions to your youth minister or other knowledgeable Christian.

3. Who is the wisest person you know?

Why does this person get your vote? Give as many reasons as you can think of.

4. Both Solomon and Jesus said that giving in to a "little" sin can lead to great failings (see Eccles. 9:18; Luke 12:1,2). What does the word *sin* mean? (Look it up in a Bible dictionary if you have one.)
   What are common sins for people your age?
   What provisions has God made to deal with sin?
   Here are some verses for you to contemplate: John 3:18; 5:24; 10:28; Romans 3:20-26; 5:9,17; 8:1; 1 Corinthians 1:30; James 4:17; 1 John 1:9.

5. In the Bible, love is more than just an emotion. It is the Christian's way of life. What are some specific and simple acts of love that you could do to make life better around the house?

6. Words—wise ones and foolish ones—can pack a lot of punch. Watch thirty minutes of TV. Write down the number of commercials you see and the basic message of each.
   In what ways are the ads using words to try and sway your thinking?
   In what ways are they using images?
   Do you think the words and images present the truth about each product?
   What principles about influencing people can you learn from these ads?
   Which ones could a Christian use to have a positive impact on other people's thinking?

7. Take a gander at Luke 14:28-33. In what ways do each of these two stories relate to the Christian commitment?

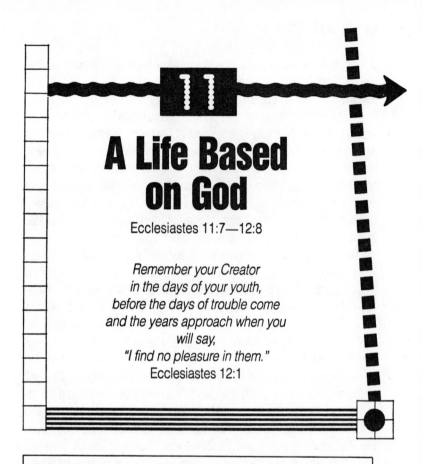

A Life Based on God

Ecclesiastes 11:7—12:8

Remember your Creator
in the days of your youth,
before the days of trouble come
and the years approach when you
will say,
"I find no pleasure in them."
Ecclesiastes 12:1

Complete commitment to God is the essential element that produces fulfillment during every stage of life.

Solomon used the word *meaningless* more than 30 times in Ecclesiastes. Here is a list of the things he considered to be meaningless, given in the order they appear in Ecclesiastes: everything; all things done under the sun; pleasure; achievement; wisdom; work; leaving possessions to a successor; the pain, grief and worry of work; gathering and storing wealth; death; envy; loneliness; working too hard; advancement; money; lack of contentment; unfulfilled desire; the few days of life; the laughter of fools; the Teacher's own life; respect for the wicked dead; punishment for the righteous and reward for the wicked; and finally, our own lives.

Many of the things on the list seem desirable. If a person were able to build a life the way a house is built, wouldn't he or she build with bricks of pleasure, achievement, wisdom, advancement, wealth, laughter and so forth? Why did Solomon consider these things to be of so little value? He probably felt that way because they are temporary. A life built with these bricks will fall down, because the bricks don't last. Money is meaningless, for instance, because it accomplishes nothing of eternal duration.

God is also mentioned in Ecclesiastes more than thirty times. Here is some of what the Teacher says about Him: He has laid a heavy burden (life) on people; He allows us to eat and find enjoyment; He gives wisdom, knowledge and happiness to the good, the task of gathering wealth to the wicked; He can be pleased; He makes everything beautiful in its time; He has set eternity in our hearts; everything He does will endure forever; He does what He does so people will revere Him; God will call us to account; God will judge the righteous and the wicked; God tests us; He should be listened to; He is in heaven; He dislikes foolishness; He can be angered and may destroy our works; He inspires awe; God gives life; He gives wealth and possessions and enables us to enjoy them; He keeps us occupied with gladness; He may prevent a person from enjoying wealth; He can make life straight or crooked; He can make times good or bad; He is to be feared; He will cut short the days of those who don't fear Him; the righteous and the wise and what they do are in God's hands; God has made all things.

Notice how often the idea of the eternal and infinite is brought into this list: He has given us a sense of eternity; everything He does lasts forever; He will judge us as we enter into eternity; He made the universe; He is in heaven beyond our finite realm; His control over us and over events testifies to His infinite power and majesty.

To get back to the house analogy, God should be the foundation on which we build our lives. He alone is able to sustain us forever.

If God is not our foundation, then money, fame, illness, power, life and death have no lasting meaning. But when God is our base, then every little detail of life has eternal significance.

This is why Solomon wrote Ecclesiastes. As he looked around and saw the deadly error he had slipped into in his old age (idolatry) and the vain efforts of others, he came to realize what a horrible mistake humanity has made. There is no point to our self-centeredness and our materialism. The one who puts his or her faith in anything other than Almighty God is chasing the wind.

The Ticket

So we come back to the Teacher's original question that he voiced way back in the third verse of the first chapter: "What does man gain from all his labor at which he toils under the sun?" Our first reaction may be to say, "Zippo, pal. Zero. The Big *O*. Nada-rooski." That reply may not be quite right, but even if it was, there is a much more interesting answer: "It doesn't matter."

That's right. It makes no difference whether we gain nothing or gain the whole world. Even if we could gain the whole universe with its zillions of galaxies, it would still be one squashed banana compared to what awaits us in God's empire.

But this dream becomes real only for those who gain admission. What is the ticket to heaven and how much does it cost?

Jesus said, "For whoever wants to save his life will lose it, but whoever loses his life for me and for the gospel will save it. What good is it for a man to gain the whole world, yet forfeit his soul? Or what can a man give in exchange for his soul?" (Mark 8:35-37). In one breath the Lord has given us three insights that confirm the basic truths of the book of Ecclesiastes.

First, if we center our hopes and dreams on ourselves, we will lose everything. Conversely, if we center ourselves on God, we will gain true life. Second, even if we did gain the whole world or even the whole universe, what is that if we lose our eternal soul? Finally, all of creation isn't enough to buy the admission of one soul into heaven.

Our ticket to heaven, as you know, is the Lord Jesus Christ. The cost is our life.

Meanwhile . . .
You may say, "Heaven will be great, but I still gotta live on this planet today. What should I be doing meanwhile?" You should be enjoying the life and blessings God has given you, just as Solomon has recommended several times. We'll see as we study this next part of Ecclesiastes that Solomon offers a few suggestions for finding happiness in life. But his main advice is that we always keep our mind on God.

> Light is sweet,
>> and it pleases the eyes to see the
>> sun.
> However many years a man may live,
>> let him enjoy them all.
> But let him remember the days of
>> darkness,
>> for they will be many.
>> Everything to come is meaningless.
>> Ecclesiastes 11:7,8

In the Scripture, *light* often is a synonym for *life*. For example, "In him was life, and that life was the light of men. The light shines in the darkness, but the darkness has not understood it" (John 1:4,5).

"Life is sweet," says the Teacher. His wish is that we will enjoy all the years of our lives. But, he cautions us, be mindful of the grave shrouded in darkness at the end of the road. The days of the grave will be many and meaningless, at least in the Teacher's point of view. However, as John 1:4,5 reveals, Christ's light can shine brightly and conquer even spiritual darkness.

> Be happy, young man, while you are
>> young,
>> and let your heart give you joy in the
>> days of your youth.
> Follow the ways of your heart
>> and whatever your eyes see,

> *but know that for all these things*
> *God will bring you to judgment.*
> Ecclesiastes 11:9

The person who is mindful of the divine appointment that he or she has with Almighty God will not live like the person who rejects God. It's like the first time you had to see the dentist. Can you remember how thoroughly you brushed your teeth? The fear of the dentist brought home the need for good oral hygiene. It was not an irrational fear. It was a healthy respect for the consequences of not caring for your teeth the way you should. That fear and respect is magnified a thousand times in this thought: "If we deliberately keep on sinning after we have received the knowledge of the truth, no sacrifice for sins is left, but only a fearful expectation of judgment and of raging fire that will consume the enemies of God" (Heb. 10:26,27). If you honestly desire to enjoy a solid, purposeful friendship with Jesus, it is essential that you make deliberate commitment to not only avoid sin but also to uphold what is right. A casual attitude is dangerous.

One of the great surprises of becoming a Christian and behaving like a child of God is the discovery that it is actually fun to be good! There is no guilt, no regret and lots of joy. Anyone who has been walking with the Lord for a few years can look back and see the benefits of being good and the sorrows of being foolish. The fact that Satan has managed to convince the world that sin is forever fun is the biggest ripoff of all time.

There is no need for the Christian to reject money, pleasure, laughter, achievement or any of the other "bricks" we talked about. These things are good if handled in a godly fashion. The Bible has plenty to say about all these parts of life. You can look them up in a good concordance and find plenty of straight talk on how to enjoy them as God wants us all to do.

Imprint God on Your Life

> *So then, banish anxiety from your*
> *heart*

> *and cast off the troubles of your body,*
> *for youth and vigor are meaningless.*
>   Ecclesiastes 11:10

Again with the meaningless! But he's right; remembering that anything temporary is like mist in the hot sun compared to eternity, we know that youth and energy aren't of much value. Those who anxiously cling to their youthfulness as the answer to life are clutching at evaporating water.

The Teacher spends the next several verses discussing the nature of youth and old age. He begins with a sage observation that you should pin to the inside of your locker door:

> *Remember your Creator*
> *in the days of your youth,*
> *before the days of trouble come*
> *and the years approach when you*
> *will say,*
> *"I find no pleasure in them."*
>   Ecclesiastes 12:1

The word that Solomon used for *remember* can also be translated as *imprint*. Imprint God on your life. This sort of remembering goes far beyond merely recalling that there is a God out there somewhere. It means to direct your thinking and actions always toward Him, to decisively live for Him. It means to press His nature into yours. This is what Paul meant when, after telling his readers to always be thinking about things that are true, noble, right, pure, lovely, admirable, excellent and praiseworthy, he said, "Whatever you have learned or received or heard from me, or seen in me—put it into practice. And the God of peace will be with you" (Phil. 4:9). Put it into action. Imprint it in your heart. If you do, the God of peace will be with you.

How do you imprint God on your life? Try these ideas:

• Read your Bible every day.

- Go to Bible studies and prayer meetings.
- Talk to God, think about Him often.
- Think about specific ways He should be involved in all your interests. For example, how should He be influencing your relationship with your girlfriend or boyfriend?
- Hang around with Christians.
- Seek His guidance.
- Read Christian books.

These simple suggestions, if turned into habits, will help establish a growing, maturing relationship between you and the Lord.

Pass the Liver Pills, Martha

Ecclesiastes 12:2-5 talks about the problems of being old. Solomon presents a poetic allegory—old age is like a tumbledown house. The "keepers of the house tremble" (the arms and hands get the shakes), the "strong men stoop" (the legs and shoulders get the bends), the "grinders cease because they are few" (start shopping for dentures), those "looking through the windows grow dim" (get a magnifying glass and reading lamp), the "doors to the street are closed and the sound of grinding fades" (if it won't go through a straw you can't eat it) and men "rise up at the sound of birds, but all their songs grow faint" (even if they're getting harder to hear, those stupid sparrows keep waking you up.).

Old people have to be "afraid of heights and of dangers in the streets" (fear of falling and vulnerability to crime). When "almond trees blossom" (the hair grows white) and "the grasshopper drags itself along" (the energy is gone and the world seems chilly) and "desire is no longer stirred" (sexual desire is a memory), then the person "goes to his eternal home and mourners go about the streets."

Remember him—before the silver cord
is severed,
or the golden bowl is broken;
before the pitcher is shattered at the spring,

> *or the wheel broken at the well,*
> *and the dust returns to the ground it*
> *came from,*
> *and the spirit returns to God who*
> *gave it.*
> Ecclesiastes 12:6,7

Remember God when you are young and vigorous and remember Him when you are old and a bit shopworn. Don't forget, God is the foundation and Jesus is the rock on which we can build our house.

Whether you are young or old, life presents an opportunity to know and serve the Lord. God rewards those who follow Him all the days of their lives. Listen to what these New Testament writers said about this:

> *Let us not become weary in doing good, for at the proper time*
> *we will reap a harvest if we do not give up.*
> Galatians 6:9

> *Let us run with perseverance the race marked out for us. Let*
> *us fix our eyes on Jesus, the author and perfecter of our faith,*
> *who for the joy set before him endured the cross, scorning its*
> *shame, and sat down at the right hand of the throne of God.*
> *Consider him who endured such opposition from sinful men,*
> *so that you will not grow weary and lose heart.*
> Hebrews 12:1-3

Beyond the Grave

> *"Meaningless! Meaningless!" says the*
> *Teacher.*
> *"Everything is meaningless!"*
> Ecclesiastes 12:8

Solomon repeats the statement he made at the beginning of Ecclesiastes. There, it seemed a cry of frustration. Here, after all the folly and injustice and sadness, it sounds like profanity. The word *profane* literally means "before the temple." In other words, something not a part of God's kingdom. The meaningless life—the empty, hollow, shallow, insignificant existence—is alien to God's kingdom. It is a profanity. The life God gives to anyone who comes to Him is purposeful and fulfilling.

I suspect that shortly after he was ushered through the gates of heaven, Solomon was shouting, "Meaning! Meaning! It all makes sense!"

1. Solomon spoke about the young and the aged. List some practical ways a person in high school could effectively serve the Lord.

   Think of some ways you might be able to serve the Lord when your body is old.

   What career might you like to pursue in the years before you grow old?

   In what ways could you serve the Lord on that job?

   In what ways might that job tend to hinder your Christian service?

2. Do you know any old people in your church fellowship? In what ways do they seem to have a better relationship with God than you might have?

   List some ideas for bringing the youth group and the older folks closer together.

3. I said at the beginning of this chapter that you should pin this verse to the inside of your locker door: "Remember your Creator in the days of your youth, before the days of trouble come and the years approach when you will say, 'I find no pleasure in them'" (Eccles. 12:1).

   Do you think your commitment to God will deepen as you grow older, or are you afraid it might fade?

   List the things that might cause you to fall away from God and the things you could do to counteract them.

4. In this chapter there is a list of things you can do to "imprint" God on your life. Design a chart that schedules time for you to do each of the things on the list during the next week or two.

5. On the list mentioned in number four, it says "Read Christian books." Besides the Bible, what is your favorite Christian book?

   Go to a Christian bookstore or your church library and pick up a couple of paperbacks to enjoy.

6. It was said that the meaningless life is empty, hollow, shallow, and insignificant existence. The life God gives to anyone who comes to Him is purposeful and fulfilling. In what ways has God made your life purposeful and fulfilling?

   What will you do to discover more of God's purpose for your life?

7. "Meaning! Meaning! It all makes sense!" That may have been Solomon's cry as he beheld the answers before his eyes in heaven. What questions would you like to ask God when you see Him?

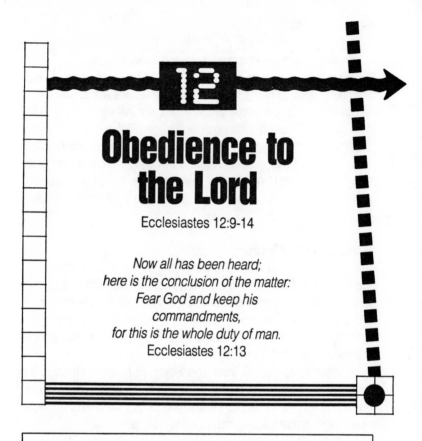

Obedience to the Lord

Ecclesiastes 12:9-14

Now all has been heard;
here is the conclusion of the matter:
Fear God and keep his
commandments,
for this is the whole duty of man.
Ecclesiastes 12:13

In the final analysis, the question facing us in the book of Ecclesiastes is whether or not we are willing to live in obedience to the Lord.

If the book of Ecclesiastes is like a dark and twisted cave, the portion we are about to explore is the light at the end of the tunnel, freshened by the sweet air of the open outdoors. In our search through Ecclesiastes we've stumbled across a few rocky points along the way and knocked our skulls against some of the Teacher's harder sayings, but our pockets and backpacks are filled to overflowing with the treasure of discovered wisdom.

There remains the happy duty of spending the loot.

Having helped us investigate the dim nature of life without God, Solomon leads us to the surface and to the cave's exit. The exit is really an entrance, a portal to the world of meaning and joy. Solomon taps his walking stick against a large billboard posted at the mouth of the cave. The light hurts our eyes until they adjust to the brightness. But we can read the words. They say, "Now all has been heard; here is the conclusion of the matter: Fear God and keep his commandments, for this is the whole duty of man" (Eccles. 12:13).

Solomon's Qualifications

Ecclesiastes is a hard book to read. It's not that it's too long or that the words are too big or the logic too tough to follow. No, it's hard to read because it asks us to examine our lives and view them in such a dismally pessimistic way. According to the Teacher, our goals and dreams, even our lives are pointless and of no value. Few people like reading such depressing news!

Nonetheless, truth is truth and Solomon has a lock on it. It's impossible for an honest person to argue his conclusions. To be sure no one tries, he begins the last part of his book with a list of the qualifications that allowed him to speak with authority:

Not only was the Teacher wise, but also he imparted knowledge to the people. He pondered and searched out and set in order many proverbs. The Teacher searched to find just the right words, and what he wrote was upright and true.
Ecclesiastes 12:9,10

Solomon states the fact that he was a wise man. He was not bragging or puffing himself up, he was acknowledging God's gift to him. Moreover, he didn't keep the wisdom to himself for his own personal gain. He sought to share it with all who would listen. He was the Teacher.

Solomon did three things to accomplish his mission. First, he "pondered" wisdom. He carefully weighed and measured every idea and set his mind to the investigation of truth and meaning. Second, he "searched out" wisdom. Solomon used his eyes and ears to discover new thoughts and ideas. He seemed to say that he set a goal and then embarked upon a planned search for the data he needed to reach it. Finally, he "arranged proverbs" to transfer his insights to others. His proverbs would serve as proof of his wisdom or lack of it. If they were accepted and praised by others, then his wisdom would be endorsed. His proverbs, as you know, gave him the reputation of being the wisest man in the world.

His reputation wasn't easily won. He "searched to find just the right words," a process that was essential to communicating his intended meaning. A proper word is like a bullet that passes through the bull's-eye of a target; the wrong word can backfire or ricochet off course to cause injury.

Solomon also made sure his thoughts conformed to the strict standards of truth. Great lies have swayed entire nations and started world wars. Solomon would have none of that. His words were true and upright.

Solomon's Words
The words of the wise are like goads, their collected sayings like firmly embedded nails—given by one Shepherd.
Ecclesiastes 12:11

A goad is a long, nasty stick used to jab some purpose and meaning into the life of an obstinate animal. "We will go now," says the animal's caretaker. "We shall not," replies the malingering beast. "Yes, we shall," responds the implanted stick—and off we go.

Unpleasant as they are, Solomon's insights into life serve to motivate us to action. Wisdom is never intended to be an exercise of the intellect only; it is meant to change lives in dynamic and radical ways.

When the Bible, God's wisdom, is put into practice, it transforms the believer. To be transformed implies not only a change of outside appearance but of the inner substance. "Therefore, if anyone is in Christ, he is a new creation; the old has gone, the new has come!"

(2 Cor. 5:17). If we are to learn from Ecclesiastes, we must be willing to put some wheels underneath us and get moving.

The collected sayings of the wise are also like "firmly embedded nails." In Solomon's day, people staked their tents to the ground with long spikes called nails. The nails prevented the tents from blowing away at the first stiff gust. The Bible's wisdom is the tent pegs of the Christian's life, providing spiritual stability and security. A person who practices the wisdom in God's Word won't wander away from the truth.

The words of the wise are "given by one Shepherd." It is of critical importance that those who look at the Bible understand that it is truly God's Word. It is not a man-made invention. "All Scripture is God-breathed and is useful for teaching, rebuking, correcting and training in righteousness, so that the man of God may be thoroughly equipped for every good work" (2 Tim. 3:16). All Scripture, including Ecclesiastes, is inspired by the Lord.

A shepherd was one who used both goads and nails in the line of duty. Goads to lead the sheep and nails to pitch the tent by the streams and meadows necessary for animals' benefit. Psalm 23, written by Solomon's dad, says, "The Lord is my shepherd, I shall not be in want" (v. 1). Jesus proclaimed, "I am the good shepherd. The good shepherd lays down his life for the sheep" (John 10:11). Our Lord is our protector and provider. His guidance is found in the Bible.

A Warning

Be warned, my son, of anything in addition to them.
Of making many books there is no end, and much study wearies the body. Ecclesiastes 12:12

The first part of this verse is similar to Revelation 22:18,19:

I warn everyone who hears the words of the prophecy of this book: If anyone adds anything to them, God will add to him the plagues described in this book. And if anyone takes words away from this book of prophecy, God will take away from him his share in the tree of life and in the holy city, which are described in this book.

No one is to mess with the wisdom of God's Word. These passages are often used to combat Christian cults, organizations that twist the meaning of God's Word and often claim their own books are equal or superior to the Bible.

The second part of Ecclesiastes 12:12 is a great one to try on your mom during school exam time. I tried it, but it didn't work. Alas, some people fail to see the great wisdom in God's Word.

Solomon's Conclusion

Now all has been heard;
here is the conclusion of the matter:
Fear God and keep his
commandments,
for this is the whole duty of man.
For God will bring every deed into
judgment,
including every hidden thing,
whether it is good or evil.
Ecclesiastes 12:13,14

This is the treasure buried deep within that has now been brought to light. Do we want meaning in life? Solomon tells us what to do and why. His message in Ecclesiastes can be summarized: Center your life on God and live like He has told you to. Do this because everything you do, everything you are, is of meaning and significance to God. His coming judgment will prove this to be true.

The "whole duty of man" is to fear God and to obey Him. The concept of fearing God is mentioned many times in the Old Testament and several times in the New. Solomon used it often in the book of Proverbs. For example: "The fear of the Lord is the beginning of knowledge, but fools despise wisdom and discipline" (Prov. 1:7); "To fear the Lord is to hate evil" (8:13); and "The fear of the Lord is the beginning of wisdom" (9:10).

Jesus said, "I tell you, my friends, do not be afraid of those who kill the body and after that can do no more. But I will show you whom you should fear: Fear him who, after the killing of the body, has power to throw you into hell. Yes, I tell you, fear him" (Luke 12:4,5). The only One who has the power to throw a person into hell is God. Jesus emphasized that we should respect and stand in awe of the One who possesses that power. Jesus immediately went to encourage his friends by reminding them that God does care for them. Jesus explained that only those who deny Him must fear hell.

It should be clear from our study of Ecclesiastes that to fear God means to give Him your heart, to center your life on Him. If a person really esteems, admires and heeds the Lord, commitment to God naturally follows. That sort of commitment obviously demands obedience to the Lord.

The fear of God is what brings us into the proper relationship with our Creator. Since that relationship is what gives our lives meaning, the fear of God and obedience to Him is the answer to the Teacher's cry of "Meaningless!"

Solomon reminds us that God is our judge. He will "bring every deed into judgment, including every hidden thing, whether it is good or evil" (Eccles. 12:14). This means that everything in life is important—nothing goes unnoticed or without consequence. The King takes each one of us, even in our lowest moments, very seriously! He loves us and He is involved in our existence.

Spending the Loot

By sticking with our study of life in the book of Ecclesiastes, we have come to the treasure chest of great value: the meaningful life. Now we know how to find purpose, joy, significance, importance and all the other aspects of a meaningful life. We find them as we find God. A good case could be made that all the things people look for and long for in life—no matter if they are in high school or nearing the end of the road—are symptoms of a need for meaning. Meaning is the great treasure offered to all who would come and take it at the side of Jesus.

It is not enough to know about the gift of meaning. A paycheck is no good while it is still in the envelope. I encourage you to enjoy life by renewing your dedication to our Lord.

1. Read Proverbs 2:1—3:12. Underline all the subjects in this passage that were touched on in the book of Ecclesiastes.

2. Read Proverbs 3:13-18. Solomon wrote these verses. List the positive virtues of wisdom found in this passage and summarize them in a short paragraph.

3. What significant things did you learn from your study of Ecclesiastes?

    What changes have you felt the need to make in your life because of what you have learned?

4. One of the things that seemed to set Solomon apart from the crowd was his ability to glean insights from all he saw, thought and felt. What does the word *insight* mean?

    Have you ever experienced a sudden flash of insight, an "Aha!" reaction to something you've seen, heard or read (perhaps Ecclesiastes)?

    How did you feel about yourself when this insight occurred to you?

    How do you suppose you could develop the ability to have insights more often?

    How do you think Solomon developed the gift of wisdom that God gave him?

5. Solomon's words were upright and true, according to Ecclesiastes 12:10. Do people think of you as upright and true?

    Do others trust your words?

    What standards would you like people to see in your behavior?

6. Read Ecclesiastes 12:11 again. As you have listened to the Word

of God at Bible studies or read it for yourself, in what ways have you felt "goaded" or "nailed" by Scripture?

When you discover something about yourself that does not measure up to the standards set in God's Word, how do you respond, pessimistically or optimistically?

What might a person do to begin to change from a pessimist to an optimist?

7. How does Solomon's pronouncement that God will judge you make you feel?

What things could you do to gain reward in heaven?